THE
HYBRID
TEACHER

THE
HYBRID
TEACHER

*Using Technology
to Teach In Person
and Online*

EMMA PASS

WILEY

Jossey-Bass
A Wiley Imprint
111 River St, Hoboken, NJ 07030
www.josseybass.com

Jossey-Bass books and products are available through most bookstores. To contact Jossey-Bass
directly, call our Customer Care Department within the U.S. at 800–956–7739, outside the U.S. at +1
317 572 3986, or fax +1 317 572 4002.

Wiley also publishes its books in a variety of electronic formats and by print-on-demand. Some
material included with standard print versions of this book may not be included in e-books or in print-
on-demand. If this book refers to media such as a CD or DVD that is not included in the version you
purchased, you may download this material at http://booksupport.wiley.com. For more information
about Wiley products, visit www.wiley.com.

Library of Congress Cataloging-in-Publication Data is Available:

ISBN 9781119789857 (paperback)
9781119789864 (ePDF)
9781119789871 (ePub)

COVER DESIGN: PAUL MCCARTHY
COVER ART: © JACEK KITA | GETTY IMAGES

FIRST EDITION

SKY100273850_060121

Contents

About the Author

Emma Pass is a middle school language arts teacher at a hybrid school in Fort Collins, Colorado. She is the creator of Tag: personalized spelling lists, and works as an educational technology consultant and professional development provider with her own company Empowered Edu.

EMPOWERED·edu

Acknowledgments

A huge thank you to all of my colleagues and friends who I interviewed for this book: Kate Stevens, Tory Wilson, Stacy Denham, Lindsey Mater, Hannah McGrath, Amie Sharp, Aubrey Yeh, Cole Zawaski, Theresa Hoover, and Emma Chitters.

Sam Nagel, who kept Empowered Edu afloat when we were drowning in work.

Cleo Masia, Meraki Designs, for helping to make my work look nice

Betsey Martens, Iris Writing, for quick, clean, and kind copyediting, plus never ending support.

Izzy Martens, marketing advice and general support.

Will Pass for endless edits and enthusiasm.

Before We Begin

HOW TO USE THIS BOOK (PRINT)

I am an English teacher and therefore love physical, paper books. I love to hold them, smell them, gaze upon them as they sit peacefully upon my bookshelf. However, this is a book about technology, and technology is fast paced, flexible, and alive.

Nearly every page of this book has a live link for you to explore, which is very hard to do on paper, which is why I've created an interactive webpage to accompany this book that you can access at hybridteacherresource.com. The links are also available on this book's page on www.wiley.com.

I recommend you highlight, underline, and annotate galore in the print version, and when you get to a link you want to explore, visit the webpage on your computer to find and follow the link. They should be easy to find as they are organized in the same chapter and subsection headings.

Then, be sure to bookmark your favorite tools to use later!

"FREEMIUM"

As I mentioned, this book is chock full of links to educational technology (EdTech) resources. Often I see myself as less of a writer and more of a librarian or curator of EdTech tools, and this book is a collection of my current favorites.

Because the people who make these tools often do it as a means of employment, most tools have some premium version that you can buy to unlock additional features or products.

However, because I am myself a teacher and know all too well the reality of teaching without a classroom budget and spending out of pocket, EVERY tool I mention in this book has a FREE version. In fact, almost every tool I use in my own classroom is the free version.

If you have a sizable classroom budget, why not upgrade and support the education technology industry? If you have a sizable heart and pockets, consider donating to Donors Choose (www.donorschoose.org) to help other teachers upgrade as well.

Disclaimer: I am not sponsored or paid by any of these companies to promote their products.

GLOSSARY

These terms will help provide a foundational understanding for the content that follows.

Hybrid Learning	Refers to the place learning happens; in person and online.
Blended Learning	Refers to the tools used to conduct learning; a combination of traditional tools (i.e. books) and online tools (i.e. laptops, videos, EdTech).
Online Learning	Education that takes place entirely online.
Learning Management System (LMS)	An online platform for the facilitation of learning. Most notably the distribution and collection of student work.
Video Conferencing	An online platform where multiple people can join a call via video voice, video, or both.
Synchronous Learning	Teaching and learning occurs together, simultaneously.
Asynchronous Learning	Students access learning at different times and work through it at their own pace.
Browser	An application that allows you to access the internet. Chrome, Firefox, and Safari are examples.
Chrome Extension	Small software programs that give you additional features on any given website within your Chrome web browser.
Add-On	The "add-ons" I refer to in this book are specific to Google files such as docs, slides, and sheets. Add-ons are downloaded to your Doc, Slide, or Sheet and provide advanced functionalities.
App	A computer program that needs to be downloaded to your device (most often a phone or tablet).
Hyperlink	Similar to an address, a hyperlink directs you to a website or web-based document.

Introduction

Far and away the best prize that life offers is the chance to work hard at work worth doing.

—*Theodore Roosevelt*

THE WHY

Before I start teaching a new unit, I always try to address the "Why?" with my students. Why are we learning about this? Why will it be meaningful to you? Why will it be beneficial to your life?

For this book, I've not only asked myself the "why?" but a few more Ws too. Here is what I've come up with:

- *What:* This is a book about using technology and online pedagogy to enhance teaching and learning as a whole.

- *Who is it for:* K-12 teachers of all content areas, in brick-and-mortar, remote, and hybrid schools.

- *How might it be used:*

1. Emergency Preparedness

   I was approached to write this book in the height of the COVID-19 pandemic, when millions of schools globally shut their doors in order to reduce the transmission of disease and save lives.

   When it comes to safety, schools regularly prepare and practice for emergency scenarios. I imagine schools will now begin to adopt and regularly practice "emergency remote learning" to be prepared for future disease outbreaks, natural disasters, or any other number of unforeseen circumstances.

   This is a guide for them.

2. Emerging Hybrid School Models

   Although many teachers, students, parents, and administrators (rightfully) struggled with adapting to emergency remote or hybrid learning during the COVID-19 pandemic, I hope some innovative educators were able to see beyond the struggle to the benefits of hybrid learning for certain student populations, and new hybrid schools models will begin emerging in districts across the country.

This is a guide for them.

3. Educational Technology Benefits Everyone

In a 2016 Arizona State University study on educational technology (EdTech), researchers found that the use of EdTech in teaching and learning "can have considerable positive impacts on student performance, and efforts to adopt new educational technologies in the classroom will be rewarded."

Although this book is focused on teaching in a hybrid model, the tools and techniques can be applied to most learning environments.

The study also found that the biggest barrier to success in the implementation of EdTech is providing teachers with the necessary professional development.

This is a guide for you.

Bring it back to the building

If you teach full time in a "brick-and-mortar" classroom, look for these sections, where I explain how an online tool, resource, or strategy could be used in a traditional classroom model.

MY WHY

My first teaching job was as a 6th-grade English teacher in Las Vegas, Nevada. My years there were easily the most challenging and rewarding of my life. My love for those first students of mine resonates throughout my entire body. My students came from the most diverse (in the true sense of the word) backgrounds imaginable. They were Black, White, Latinx, European, African, and Asian.

They were the children of wealthy surgeons as well as single parents who worked the night shift at Burger King. Some of my students had boats that they would take out on Lake Mead, while others were homeless. Our school was a magnet school for the deaf and hard of hearing, and we had a number of students who were Syrian refugees.

Meeting the needs of such a diverse and large group (I taught nearly 200 students per year) was an impossible task. However, I thank my lucky stars every day that our school was awarded a grant in my first year of teaching to receive 1-1 Chromebook devices. (Meaning each student had access to their own device that they were able to use in school and take home.)

Because I had little other experience teaching, I threw myself entirely into learning how to use educational technology to engage my students and differentiate instruction to meet the needs of as many learners as possible. I was also incredibly lucky to have a teacher-mentor, Larenda Norman, who supported me and encouraged me to continue learning.

A few years later when my husband had the opportunity to cover a European news circuit, we jumped at the opportunity to live in London. There, I had another lucky break in meeting my next mentor, Andy Caffrey, with whom I traveled the country and continent working as an educational technology consultant, teaching and training other teachers to use technology in their classrooms.

I currently live in my home state of Colorado, where I still work part time as an EdTech consultant through my consulting company, Empowered Edu. I also teach 7th- and 8th-grade language arts at PSD Global Academy (PGA), a public hybrid school in which students spend half of their time learning in person and half of their time learning from home.

I wanted to start with my story because the perspective of this book comes entirely from these experiences. A lot of what I write about comes not from research or interviews but the time I've spent with students.

Everything I do in education is for them.

A NOTE ON ACCESS AND EQUITY

I want to address the privilege assumed in this book.

My experiences in hybrid teaching are based largely on my current position as a teacher at PGA. We live in a well-funded, predominantly White city where we are able to provide laptop devices, 1-1, to all of the students in our school and district.

Further, many of the students who come to our hybrid school have a stay-at-home or work-from-home parent to support and encourage their learning during online/remote days. There are exceptions, but we are ultimately teaching in a position of great privilege.

This type of digital access and support is not a reality for many schools and districts that are disproportionately made up of low-income, rural, Black, Latinx, and/or Native American populations.

I say this to emphasize the existence of a "digital divide" in our country, which needs to be bridged so that we provide access to technology, Wi-Fi, professional development, and after-school/at-home support to every student, school, and district nationwide.

Shining a light on the issue is only the first step, and it is not enough. People in a position of privilege can choose to simply look away because it does not affect them. If you are in such a position, choose to turn toward the light, then act. There are several immediate steps we can take to help:

- Sign a petition on Change.org demanding action to provide internet access to low income families.

- Contact your state representatives to request additional funding to public education, specifically to address the digital divide.

- Donate to ConnectHomeUSA.org, a company working to bridge the digital divide in government assisted housing, or to DonorsChoose.org, where you can provide resources directly to teachers and classrooms nationwide.

I have done my best to explore practical and tangible options for addressing access to technology in the section "Access to Technology" in Chapter 14.

With great hope and effort, we will achieve digital access equity in our country.

Teach on,

Emma

RESOURCES

Items in **bold** in the text are listed here in the Resources.

2016 Arizona State University study on educational technology—http://files.eric.ed.gov/fulltext/ED577147.pdf.

Chapter 1
Synchronous and Asynchronous Learning

I never teach my pupils; I only attempt to provide the conditions in which they can learn.

—Albert Einstein

When we talk about teaching and learning, especially in the context of a digital learning environment, we are typically thinking about it in one of two ways:

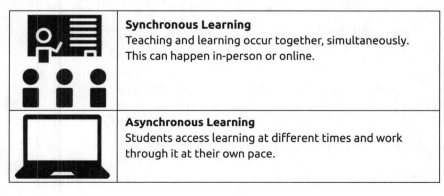

	Synchronous Learning Teaching and learning occur together, simultaneously. This can happen in-person or online.
	Asynchronous Learning Students access learning at different times and work through it at their own pace.

Synchronous learning is what typically happens in a traditional brick-and-mortar school; it's what we think of when we hear "teaching." The teacher stands in front of the class and delivers instruction, and the students receive the information simultaneously. Then students practice and apply their learning within the time constraints of the class period.

However, it's important to note that synchronous learning can also be conducted remotely over a video conferencing platform like Zoom or Google Meet in a remote or hybrid learning scenario.

In contrast, asynchronous learning is typically prebuilt and posted for students on a learning management system (LMS) to access within the time constraints of a day, week, or unit.

Many 100% online schools are entirely asynchronous, where students have access to the entirety of their prebuilt course work, unit, or module, and they work through it at their own pace.

Hybrid schools often use a combination of both. Our PSD Global Academy (PGA) middle school schedule, for example, follows this system for delivering instruction:

Monday	Tuesday	Wednesday	Thursday	Friday
Remote Asynchronous	On-Campus Synchronous	Remote or On-Campus Asynchronous	On-Campus Synchronous	Remote Asynchronous

However, there are other methods for delivering synchronous/asynchronous instruction that you can read about in The Administrators' Appendix. These examples are found in schools that are attempting to teach synchronously to students who are both in the classroom and at home by livestreaming their lessons (concurrent instruction).

I believe there are benefits to both synchronous and asynchronous instruction, and both should be adopted as instruction methods regardless of whether you're full-time brick and mortar, hybrid, or remote.

Chapter 2
Synchronous Learning

Good teaching is 1/4 preparation and 3/4 theatre.

—*Gail Goldwin*

Synchronous Learning
Teaching and learning occur together, simultaneously. This can happen in-person or online.

Typically, whenever we are in the classroom with our students, we are engaging in synchronous learning. However, synchronous learning can also be delivered remotely via a video conferencing platform like Zoom, Google Meet, or Skype.

At PSD Global Academy (PGA) Middle School, we typically engage in synchronous learning 2 days/week (Tuesdays and Thursdays). Those lessons are done in person at our school building. During the COVID-19 school building closures, we simply moved our classes to a video conferencing program (Google Meet), maintaining nearly the exact same schedule that we had in person.

Monday	Tuesday	Wednesday	Thursday	Friday
Remote Asynchronous	Remote Synchronous	Remote Asynchronous	Remote Synchronous	Remote Asynchronous

Although I almost always prefer in-person synchronous learning to video conferencing, having those established times during the week to meet as a class to check in, see each other's faces, and hear each other's voices felt necessary not only for our academic success, but for the social-emotional well-being of students.

I am going to assume that most teachers reading this book are comfortable with delivering synchronous instruction live/in person, so I will use the rest of this chapter to explain how synchronous teaching and learning can be adapted to an online environment.

Still, keep in mind that many of these tools and tips could also be integrated into in-person synchronous instruction when we return to the classroom. For example, see the section "The Chat Box" later in this chapter to see how I plan to use the chat box in my brick-and-mortar classroom.

CHOOSING A VIDEO CONFERENCING PLATFORM

Most schools or districts will provide you with a video conferencing platform, but if you have a choice, here are some factors worth considering:

Zoom

Pros	Cons
• Waiting rooms	• Limited features in the free version
• Private chat	• Potential security risks

Microsoft Teams

Pros	Cons
• Microsoft Teams Chat (saves communication in a chat room after the call ends)	• Limited features in the free version

Google Meet

Pros	Cons
• Simple and intuitive	• Limited features in the free version
• Google Classroom integration	

Since the initial publication of this book in June 2021, all three platforms have been working hard to meet the needs of remote educators and all three now have hand-raising, breakout rooms, and custom background features. Keep in mind, however, that all platforms are continuing to make changes and release additional features in the upcoming months, so check their websites for updated information.

At PGA, we use Microsoft Teams for our staff meetings and Google Meet to teach our students. I prefer Google Meet, and most Google products, because they are simple, easy to use, and integrate well into the "Google Ecosystem." Throughout this book I will be referencing Google Meet when I discuss video conferencing or "meeting" online.

KEY VIDEO CONFERENCING FEATURES

Regardless of what you choose to use, any video conferencing software will have these key features.

The Microphone

It is the norm in my synchronous online classes that students' microphones are muted unless they are called upon. This is essential for students to be able to focus on the content being delivered. I try to hear my students' voices as much as possible during class and will ask students to unmute their microphones throughout the lesson. We also have class discussions and small-group discussions where students are encouraged to speak.

However, all of these activities need to be done thoughtfully to avoid chaos. There are just too many background sounds in all of our homes (cats, kids, dogs, garbage trucks) for more than a few people to have their microphones unmuted at any one time.

I explain this to my students at the beginning of the year and also point out that keeping your microphones muted is the norm in virtual business meetings as well (so practicing will help prepare them for possible future employment).

The Camera

Similar to the microphone, the camera feature can be turned on or off.

It is wonderful to see your students' faces when teaching remotely, and I encourage my students to leave their cameras on, but I always make it optional. Some of my students are embarrassed to show their rooms or houses, some don't have the luxury of learning in a private space, some have anxiety about being on camera, and to be honest, it can be really distracting to see your own face when you are trying to concentrate on a lesson. Whatever the reason, if a student doesn't want to turn their camera on, I don't make them.

Cameras on? Or cameras optional?

The increase in remote learning because of COVID-19 has led to a heated debate in the online learning community. Do we require students to turn their cameras on for class? Or let it be optional?

First, we need to consider the data and privacy circumstances. Is the class being recorded? If so, where is that recording going to be accessible? It's always a good idea to check with your IT department about data and privacy compliance.

Personally, I let cameras be optional in my online classes and try to engage my students in other ways (see "Synchronous Instruction"). Although I love to see their faces, I understand that it can be uncomfortable to see your own face while trying to pay attention to class, and more than that, uncomfortable to let your fellow classmates see into your room or home.

The Chat Box

Every video conferencing tool will have a chat box. Because speaking is more limited in online synchronous learning, I frequently use the chat box to get feedback from my students and keep them engaged.

Using the chat box for student participation during class has been one of the greatest silver linings I found when teaching synchronously over Google Meet. Some of my students who were very reserved and reluctant to partici-pate in brick-and-mortar class conversations were very active in the chat box and allowed me to see a completely different side to them. It also allowed me to "hear" more students' voices throughout class, without the disruption of 30 actual voices breaking out into discussion that I have to rein back in. During class over Google Meet, I can ask a question and see all my students' responses in the chat box in a matter of moments.

Aside from asking specific questions, here are the common keywords I ask my students to put into the chat box:

Here	When students first arrive, I have them type "here" into the chat box, so I can easily scroll back through their names to take attendance.
Hall Pass	If a student needs to step away from their screen, to use the bathroom or take care of a family matter, I ask them to type "hall pass" into the chat box, so I know not to call on them or to catch them up when they return.
I'm back	When a student returns, either from the bathroom or from completing an assignment on a new tab or window, I ask that they type "I'm back" or "I'm done" into the chat box, so I know they are all back in the Meet, can see my screen, and are ready to move on.
Clap clap 	If a student shares during class, I ask the rest of their classmates to give them virtual applause in the chat box, either by typing "clap clap clap" or inserting celebratory emojis.
1–10	I'll often ask students to rate something on a scale of 1–10, whether it's how they are feeling or how interesting an article was. Getting a number in the chat box is quick and easy.
Bye!	Finally, I always ask my students to say "goodbye" before they leave a virtual class by either typing in the chat box or unmuting their microphones.

Bring it back to the building

I've enjoyed using the chat box so much, in fact, that I am planning on using a chat box in the brick-and-mortar classroom as well through Backchannel Chat. **Backchannel Chat** is an online chat platform that allows teachers to create a chat room and invite students to join (without needing students to sign up or enter an email).

I plan to post the code for Backchannel at the start of each class and ask my students to use it throughout the lesson on their individual laptop devices to respond to questions and add comments. I will be moderating the chat on a tablet, locking the room if students aren't on topic.

When responding to classroom questions, sometimes students will be asked to respond in the chat, other times they will be asked to turn and talk, and often I'll give them the option to type their response *or* raise their hand and share. This allows some of my more introverted students an opportunity to contribute to the conversation when they otherwise might not.

A few added benefits to Backchannel Chat are teachers can delete individual chats, pin chats to the top of the feed, moderate messages, send students private chats, send polls, and lock the chat board to prevent further messaging.

There is a free version with less security features and a premium version with more.

Record

Another key feature that Zoom, Google Meet, and Microsoft Teams have in common is the record button.

Different schools and districts might have different interpretations of data privacy laws in whether you can record your synchronous online lesson, and it's important to check with your administrator for that direction.

If you are able to record, I would highly recommend recording all your online synchronous classes and perhaps your live brick-and-mortar classes too.

During the COVID-19 pandemic, many teachers were asked to teach simultaneously to a group of students in the classroom and a group at home (see more on this in The Administrators' Appendix). Although I don't believe this style of hybrid learning to be the most effective for teaching and learning, I do think the practice of filming and recording our lessons can have tremendous benefits.

First, consider student absences and the increased equity in being able to provide a recording of your missed lesson to a student who might not be able to make the class because they are taking care of siblings, sick parents, or

Bring it back to the building

For teachers in the brick-and-mortar classroom: I would join a Google Meet alone, share your screen, hit record, and make sure that if you are walking around during class you are using a wireless microphone to continue recording your voice (you can get wireless RF [radio frequency] microphones online or use wireless earphones like Airpods).

working to help their families. Having a recording of the class will enable that student to participate in the class (to an extent) at a later time or date, and it creates less work for the teacher in having to reteach to that student when they return to the school building.

Second, it holds you and your students accountable. There is no "he said, she said" when there is a recording of what happened in class.

Finally, it can serve as a resource for any student—present, past, or future—who might want to review the content you covered in that lesson.

You might consider editing your videos down to just include the direct instruction and putting them into a website for reference, like an FAQ page (summer project anyone?).

For teachers teaching over video conferencing, the recording process would be to simply hit record.

Digital Whiteboards

Finally, all your basic video conferencing platforms have integration with digital whiteboard tools that not only enable you to annotate live during lectures but also have features that will allow students to collaborate as they discuss, work, and brainstorm.

- **Google Jamboard**
- **Microsoft Whiteboard**
- **Zoom Whiteboard**

Each video conferencing whiteboard is designed to either be controlled only by the presenter or shared with participants to collaborate on.

Bring it back to the building

Digital whiteboards are becoming a more popular option for brick-and-mortar teaching because of the ability to save lectures, share or print the whiteboard screens, and pick up where you left off, all of which are challenging on a traditional whiteboard.

Not to mention the flexibility of digital whiteboards when used on a tablet, allowing teachers to move around the room. The teacher can project their whiteboard file to the front of the classroom, share the link with students to view on their own devices, or better yet, give students access to collaborate.

Whiteboard.fi is a great whiteboard alternative for teachers looking to give each student their own individual whiteboard to work on.

Additionally, Whiteboard.fi does not require student logins, the teacher can view all student whiteboards on a dashboard to monitor work, and "push" content onto students' whiteboards, such as practice problems.

For more on using digital whiteboards during teaching, see the "Synchronous Instruction: Lesson Breakdown" section in this chapter.

SETTING EXPECTATIONS

Teachers are accustomed to dedicating the start of every school year to establishing the norms and expectations of their class. Part of that process is introducing students to the physical classroom space and helping students understand how to navigate it.

A virtual classroom is no different. Start the year with a tour of the virtual environment, teach your students how to use the different functions of the video conferencing platform, and be sure to clearly establish your norms and expectations.

I have narrowed video conferencing norms and expectations down to three that are specific to the online environment (see Figure 2.1).

1. **You must be present and actively engaged in the lesson.**

   Being present and actively engaged means the students need to be in front of the screens for the entire lesson without physically wandering off to the bathroom or kitchen or digitally wandering off to other games or tabs. If a student really needs to step away from their computer they need to use the "hall pass" protocol described previously.

Part of that presence is how they show up in front of their cameras if they choose to turn them on. Students know they are expected to show up for their cameras as they would for school (meaning dressed appropriately and without distracting props). I remind students that if something distracting is happening behind them at home, they can always turn their cameras off.

We will be present and actively engaged in the lesson.

We will keep our mics muted unless told otherwise.

We will stay on topic in the chat box during the lesson.

Figure 2.1: Expectations.

They also need to be actively engaged in the lesson. It is all too easy for a student to join the session, turn off their camera, and wander off to do other things. My online, synchronous lessons require students to be actively responding to questions in the chat box, Pear Deck (more on this in the following section, "Synchronous Instruction: Lesson Breakdown"), or working on a collaborative document that I can see.

Students need to be engaged in this work to receive attendance or credit for the lesson.

2. **Microphones must be muted unless told otherwise.**

    See the preceding protocol.

3. **The chat box must be on topic once the lesson starts.**

    I've already mentioned the numerous ways in which I use the chat box, but students often prefer to use it as a social tool, and I always give my students an opportunity to be social at the start of class. Then, before I start the lesson, I verbally remind them of the norms and expectations, and tell them that from "this moment on" the chat box needs to be on topic.

    In order to ensure I am answering student questions, and can see if the chat box is on topic, I always join the Meet twice. I join the Meet once on my computer for delivering the lesson and a second time on my phone for monitoring the chat box.

I turn the sound on my phone all the way off, mute the microphone, turn off the camera, and just use my phone to monitor the chat.

If you have a co-teacher in your virtual room, they could be responsible for monitoring the chat and chiming in with their voice when something important comes up, but for most of us, we'll be solo and need to do both at once.

Touring the virtual environment and establishing expectations might take the entirety of your first synchronous class, and that's ok! It is better to take the time to get your systems set up correctly in the beginning, so you don't end up having to continually address behavior down the line.

Although many video conferencing software platforms have functionality that will allow you to mute or remove participants, I truly believe that clear expectations, strong relationships, and engaging lessons are the best possible behavior management strategies.

I also ask students to help contribute ideas for having a safe, fun, and successful class. You can see more on that in Chapter 9, Building Culture and Community.

SYNCHRONOUS INSTRUCTION: LESSON BREAKDOWN

Once you and your students are familiar with your online environment, and the rules, norms, and expectations are set, you are ready to start delivering synchronous lessons.

My lesson agenda usually looks something like this:

Check-in and community question (5–10 minutes)
Movement and/or mindful moment (2 minutes)
Review of norms and expectations (1 minute)
Direct instruction (15–25 minutes)
Practice or application (20–30 minutes)
Wrap-up, exit ticket, goodbye (5–10 minutes)

Before Class

10 minutes

I allow students to submit YouTube video and song links to me that they would like to see before class. I typically "open" the Google Meet 10 minutes before class starts and play the videos and songs selected by the class. (I have a YouTube playlist for each class that has their requested and approved videos on it. I "shuffle play" that play list.)

Students are also welcome to chat and socialize, in person or in the chat box, during this time.

I've noticed other educators creating digital "waiting rooms" or "welcome rooms" for their students on a Google Slide to present before class. These typically include a countdown timer to the start of class, an icebreaker question, and sometimes a challenge, activity, or "Do Now" for students to complete while they are waiting.

Using a tool like Classroom Screen (Figure 2.2) would allow you to create a preclass waiting room quickly. They have a customizable background, timers, you can write notes to your class, and include a QR code to send students off to complete various challenges and activities.

Bring it back to the building

If you are in your brick-and-mortar classroom, you can project Classroom Screen to the front of the room and use additional features like the "noise level meter" for classroom management.

Figure 2.2: Classroom Screen.

Classroom Screen's free version allows you to create and use a screen (no login required!); their premium version allows you to save screens for future use. One benefit to having the premium version is Classroom Screen's random name picker. If you have a saved screen, your student's name will already be saved in a list for easy cold calling or raffle rewards.

Community Check-In

5–10 minutes

It is nice to check in with your students at the start of each class, so they feel seen and acknowledged. I also use this as a social time for students to say

Bring it back to the building

When in the brick-and-mortar classroom, I'll use Backchannel Chat (see "Bring it back to the building" in "The Chat Box" section earlier in this chapter), Jamboard, or a Google Classroom Question for a quick community check-in at the start of each class period and I'll do a "community circle" (where we follow the same steps but speak one at a time in the circle) at the end of each class on Fridays as a nice way to reflect on the week.

whatever they want in the chat box before starting the lesson or show us their pets or props from home.

For community check-in, I always ask my students to tell me how they are feeling on a scale of 1 to 10 (obviously any scale would work), and I give them the option to elaborate and explain why. Then we do a "community question," which is a lot like an icebreaker question. For example, "If you could invent a new Hot Pocket flavor, what would it be and why?"

If we have plenty of time, I'll call on the students one at a time to unmute their microphones and speak to the group. If we are limited on time, I'll ask the students to type their answers into the chat box, and I'll narrate their responses as they come in.

I'll start the year by modeling, for a number of weeks, how the check-in and community questions go, providing a lot of support and giving the students preselected community questions. As the year goes on, I use my voice less and less, until eventually the students lead the check-in themselves, providing the question and facilitating the discussion.

Note that students always have the option to "pass" or "opt out" of any portion of community check-in.

Movement and Mindful Moment

2 minutes

After we check in, I often ask my students to move a little. Particularly when we are learning together online, it can be really difficult to sit in front of a screen all day. Again, based on the amount of time available, we'll do a number of activities:

- Participate in a movement video

  Aside from the numerous videos available on YouTube, both **GoNoodle** and **SuperMovers** have great movement videos that you can play on your shared screen during your online lesson, and the whole class can participate from home. These videos include dancing, stretching, and fitness.

- Find a movement gif

  Simply type "jumping jack gif" or "movement gif" into a Google Image search and you'll see plenty of options that you copy/paste into the start of your lesson slides and ask students to follow along.

  If you are using slides to present a lesson, you can embed these gifs at random in arbitrary intervals to ensure your students stay moving all lesson long (see Figure 2.3).

Figure 2.3: Movement gif.

- Movement Challenges

  My favorite thing to do is give students quick challenges at the start of class like, "Everybody get up and see if you can touch the ceiling!" Or "Run to your kitchen, grab a spoon, and come back and show me."

  One of my colleagues, **Mari Venturino**, asks her students to suggest a color and a shape in the chat box, and then she has them go find an object in their house that is that shape and color, "a green circle" or "purple square" for example. It is so fun to see what the students can find and bring back to show you.

  Other challenges I give include the following: do a somersault; run outside and bring back a piece of nature (rock, stick, leaf) to show me in your camera; run and touch five walls in your house, crab walk back and forth across your room three times, and get up and wiggle your whole body.

- Break-taking apps and extensions

  There are plenty of apps and extensions designed to get you out of your chair and move. **Move It Chrome Extension**, shown in Figure 2.4, allows you to set a time interval, then asks you to do movement challenges like "climb a ladder" or "wiggle your body" throughout the day. As long as you are sharing your screen, your students will see the challenges as they appear, and the whole class can follow along.

Figure 2.4: Move It Extension.

- Mindful Moment

  Once my students are energized from community check-in and/or movement activities, we do a mindful moment together to get focused for the lesson. This typically consists of me ringing a bell and everyone taking three deep breaths. Just a moment of quiet and stillness.

Another great opportunity to use gifs is to google "breathing gifs" (Figure 2.5) and find an interactive image to use in your slides. These gifs typically guide deep breathing by expanding and contracting slowly, and the goal is to sync your breathing to the movement.

Bring it back to the building

When I am in the brick-and-mortar classroom, I like to give my students a movement-based "Do Now" activity that they get started with as soon as they enter the room (gallery walk questions are a great option here), then ringing the bell is the signal to return to their seats, and take our mindful moment before we start class.

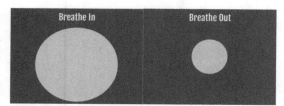

Figure 2.5: Breathing gif.

I front-load this at the beginning of the year with a lesson on the scientifically supported benefits of mindfulness in education to get student buy-in and cooperation. See more on this in Chapter 8, Social and Emotional Learning.

That moment of mindfulness is a great opportunity to set the tone for the rest of the lesson. Calm, focused, engaged.

Review of Norms and Expectations

1 minute

At this point I quickly, verbally review the norms and expectations for class (see the "Setting Expectations" section earlier in this chapter) and remind the students that from this moment on, the chat box needs to be focused on the lesson.

Direct Instruction

15–25 minutes

Direct instruction typically consists of me sharing my screen and going through a Google Slides presentation or Pear Deck presentation with my students, then demonstrating what they will be doing on their own devices.

Google Slides Presentations

Google Slides are similar to PowerPoint. I prefer Google Slides because of the simplicity, online access, and integration with other Google products, but some teachers prefer to design their direct instruction slides on PowerPoint or Prezi.

When designing direct instruction in Slides, the first thing I think about is design. Some people may consider this a frivolous first step, but the truth is, our students are more likely to engage in a lesson that looks visually appealing, bright, colorful, and fun than if they're viewing a block of black-and-white text.

I could spend hours trying to make my Slides look visually appealing, and still fall short, which is why there are a couple of amazing tools I keep bookmarked and at the ready when creating my presentations. (See Chapter 5, Keep Design in Mind, for a full list of these tools and resources.)

Once my lesson has been created using templates, images, and icons, I share my screen with the class and go through the slide deck just as I would in the classroom. The only difference is that, when I want my students to participate, I'll either ask them to type responses in the chat box or volunteer to unmute their microphone to read aloud, ask a question, or discuss.

If the lesson is relatively short, I'll just use my Slides and the chat box, before moving on to the application or practice.

Pear Deck

For any substantial lesson where I am introducing or reviewing new material, or when I am in need of formative assessment data, I use my favorite EdTech tool, **Pear Deck**.

Pear Deck allows you to add interactive questions, such as short-answer responses, multiple choice, drag and drop, drawing, and more, right into your Google Slides or PowerPoint presentations.

If you are not familiar with Pear Deck (Figure 2.6), take a moment to watch this quick introductory tutorial.

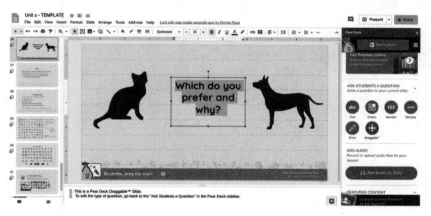

Figure 2.6: Pear Deck Google Slide add-on.

When presenting a lesson with Pear Deck, your students will be able to join the presentation on their own devices and submit their responses as you give your presentation. The best part is that you can see students as they respond in live time, quickly giving you formative assessment data of their understanding.

Although Pear Deck has a free version, I highly recommend investing in a premium account as that is what allows you to see the students' responses live. If my district didn't provide us with premium accounts, I would pay for it out of pocket—that's how much I love it and use it.

Beyond interactive questions that are compatible with Slides or PowerPoint, Pear Deck offers dozens of templates to use, or draw inspiration from, for the best possible pedagogy (see Figure 2.7). These include check-ins for understanding, summarizing the lesson, and connecting back to prior learning.

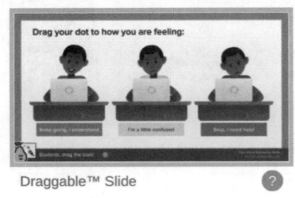

Figure 2.7: Pear Deck template.

Some of my favorite ways to use Pear Deck are:

- Starting the class with a social-emotional check-in with a draggable item on a scale.
- During the class, doing check-ins on a scale to see how they feel they are comprehending.
- At the end of the lesson, adding a one-minute summarization of what they learned through a short-answer written response (this is such powerful information!)

- My last Pear Deck slide is ALWAYS an "Express Yourself" slide. This is a blank white background with the drawing feature enabled, so students can write or draw anything they want (as long as it is school appropriate) in about one minute (see Figure 2.8). Then I always share everyone's work with the entire class.

Figure 2.8: Pear Deck "express yourself."

Again, I highly recommend Pear Deck as a tool to use for both classroom and online learning. Be sure to check out their **tutorials** or mine for a full explanation of how to get started.

Bring it back to the building

Pear Deck is particularly important when teaching synchronously online, so that you can see your students engaging in the work, even if you can't walk around the room and see what they are working on by peering over their shoulders. That said, I use Pear Deck in the brick-and-mortar classroom too! Each student is on their own device and joins via a unique code. I project the slides to the front of the room, and monitor their responses on a tablet or Chromebook as I walk around the room.

Nearpod

I use Pear Deck in my teaching, but I should also mention **Nearpod** (a tool that essentially performs the same functions). Each tool has their own benefits and drawbacks, and although I prefer Pear Deck because I find it a little cleaner, simpler, and more intuitive, the major benefit to Nearpod is the ability to see student responses in the free version.

If your school or district isn't able to pay for a premium subscription to Pear Deck, you might consider switching to Nearpod instead.

Class Kick

Class Kick is very comparable to Pear Deck and Nearpod as well. One distinct advantage it currently has is the ability to leave detailed feedback on student slides. As the teacher you can quickly leave stickers on student work, annotate with the pen tool, or type directly onto those slides.

The downside is it does not integrate with Google Slides or PowerPoint. Instead, you upload images from your computer to work from or create new lessons directly within the program.

Digital Whiteboards

As mentioned earlier in this chapter, most video conferencing tools now have digital whiteboards integrated, allowing you to annotate your presentations and for easy student collaboration during class.

A recent study by **William Beeland** found that the use of digital, interactive whiteboards in the classroom leads to increased student engagement.

I use Google Jamboard, not only for synchronous instruction, but for group work and independent practice as well.

Here are my favorite uses of Google Jamboard during direct instruction:

- Slide Annotation—If your presentation is on a Google Slide deck, you can quickly upload it to Google Jamboard via the Drive button, and pull each Google Slide onto its own whiteboard page, then you can present your lesson on Jamboard and use the marker, shape, and drawing tools to make your presentations more engaging.

- Sticky Note Response Templates—If I'd like to see all my students respond to a question in a little more of a structured format than typing their answers in the chat box, I use the sticky note feature on Google Jamboard. The first time I do this activity I'll make a Jambaord template by creating one sticky note per student, typing their name on it, and dispersing these evenly across the board. Then I make a copy of that Jamboard each time I want students to do a Jamboard response activity as shown in Figure 2.9.

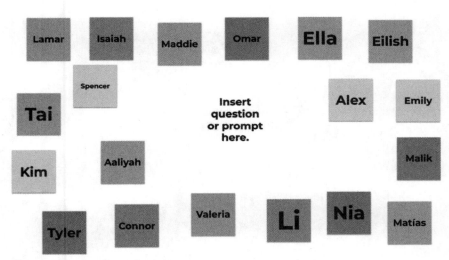

Figure 2.9: Jamboard sticky note response template.

- Would You Rather?—Jamboard makes a game of "would you rather" easy. Use a copy of your sticky note template, duplicate the whiteboard multiple times, then for each one add a "would you rather" question with a line splitting the center of the board. Students drag their sticky note to the side of the board they "would rather" and double click to type and elaborate or explain their choice.

- Check-Ins—Make a copy of your sticky note template and use that for students to quickly respond to a community check-in. To make it a little more fun, teach your student how to add an image using the Google search feature and ask them to find an image that represents how they are feeling, how their weekend was, or something they are looking forward to.

- Graffiti Wall—The concept of a "graffiti wall" in education is for students to conduct an unstructured "brain dump" about what they know (preassessment) or what they've learned (postassessment) about a topic. They can add words, quotes, pictures, and symbols to represent their understanding. A collaborative Jamboard is a great way for students to do this digitally (see Figure 2.10).

Figure 2.10: Jamboard graffiti wall example.

- Insert an Image—As I mentioned in the "Check-Ins," inserting images can be a fun way to show understanding. Teach students to insert an image quickly and easily using the Google Image search function, and ask them to place the image on their sticky note. While teaching symbols, I give students a prompt like "death" and ask them each to insert an image that commonly acts as a symbol in literature.

- Express Yourself—Just as I do in Pear Deck, to finish a lesson with Jamboard I always give my students the last minute of the lesson to "express themselves" on a blank white page. This is important not only for fun and engagement but also as a behavior management strategy. When using Jamboard as a collaborative tool, students will have the power to erase, change, and delete each other's work. I give very clear expectations on what they are supposed to do and incentivize them to get through the lesson appropriately by giving the "express yourself" jam at the end where they can go crazy. In that last minute they are allowed to erase, change, and delete to their heart's content. To make it a little more fun still, I give a countdown timer and take a screenshot of the jam at the end of the minute to post to Google Classroom. Then I change the sharing settings so students can no longer edit the Jamboard and direct them back to our Google Meet.

Sharing a Jamboard

Google Jamboard is a file type just like any other Google Doc, Slide, or Sheet, meaning you can choose to have students work on it individually or collaboratively. Most of my suggestions for Jamboard use are collaborative, but if you have an individual activity that would work great in Jamboard, simply assign it via Google Classroom and set it to "make a copy" for each student.

If you are using it in a collaborative live lesson, I suggest opening the file from your Drive, clicking the big blue share button, and using the "Get Link" option to make a shareable link for your students set to "anyone with this link can edit" as shown in Figure 2.11. Then, when you are done with the activity, go back to that same share setting and change it to anyone with the link can "view," essentially closing down the activity so students can't continue changing the file once you are done.

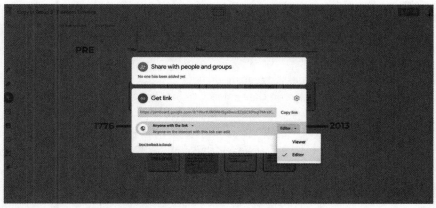

Figure 2.11: Sharing Jamboard.

Demonstrating

After delivering direct instruction, my students typically move into some individual or small-group practice for application of that skill. One of the benefits of teaching synchronously online is that your screen is already shared with the students, and it is easy to demonstrate what you want your students to do next.

Demonstrating is obvious, but I wanted to share a couple of my best practices when demonstrating work online:

- Start in Google Meet, make sure your screen is shared, and show them how to navigate from there.

- Paste any links they might need to access in the chat box (you can paste links for Google Classroom assignments there too). See Figure 2.12.

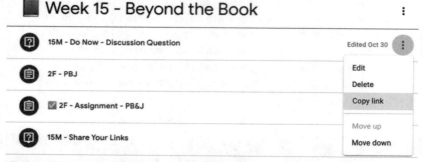

Figure 2.12: Copy link in Google Classroom.

- Using an easily accessed feature on your computer (see Chapter 14, Adapting, for how to do this) enlarge or highlight your mouse, so that students can more easily see where you are clicking. Most computers have this feature built into their accessibility tools, but as shown in Figure 2.13, you can also use a Chrome extension like **Custom Cursor for Chrome** to add additional fun. You can choose from a number of colors, shapes, and even cursors like SpongeBob, Harry Potter Cat, and a chicken nugget in the shape of a dinosaur (tell me your middle school students won't pay attention to that).

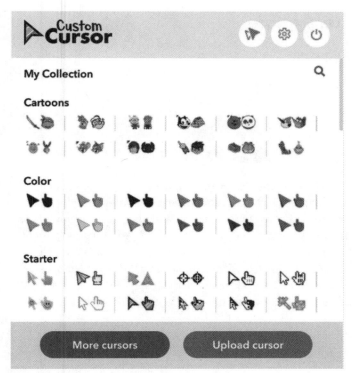

Figure 2.13: Custom Cursor.

- Tell your students they can always come back to the class video call to ask questions once they've started their work.

- Set a countdown timer on **Classroom Screen** or **Online-Stopwatch** (for fun countdowns like a candle burning or character races) and let them go!

Apply, Create, Explore

20–30 minutes

Once my students know where they are going, we spend the remainder of class time practicing or applying the content we've just learned.

There is an enormous inventory of online tools and ideas for how you might do this with your students. I've created an entire second career learning about them, and I still feel like I've barely scratched the surface of what's possible. See Chapter 4, Apply, Create, Explore, for examples and EdTech tools I like to use in both synchronous and asynchronous activities.

Specific tools and lesson ideas aside, here are some general activities I'll commonly do:

Collaborative Documents

This is an area where Google really shines. Most Google file types, like Docs, Slides, Sheets, Drawing, and Jamboard, can be shared online, and the people you share with are able to collaboratively edit or view that file.

This means that multiple students can simultaneously work on the same document on their own devices, whether they are sitting in a classroom or at home.

Because it is simply a shared file that all the students have access to, they have full control to delete or change each other's work, as well as edit and change any elements you've put into the document. You can imagine the mischievous opportunity this presents.

I typically safeguard against such shenanigans by showing students Google's **Version History**.

Because a Google file is saved second by second to the cloud, a record of these changes is saved in version history and can be reviewed by the teacher by clicking "File" and "Version History" as shown in Figure 2.14.

Figure 2.14: Google version history.

I demonstrate for my students how I can go back into their document and see any changes that have been made, even if it was deleted later and who made that change. This is usually enough to curb most undesirable behavior, and if it doesn't, I manage students on an individual basis.

Once the students know how to appropriately share a document, there is so much you can do:

- Have groups create a short presentation to share at the end of class on Google Slides.
- Collaboratively annotate an article or other text/image in Google Docs or Google Slides.
- Ask each student to contribute one Google Slide with their own summary/reflection/image, then view and comment on each other's.
- Write a **collaborative/progressive story on Google Docs**.
- Ask students to have a discussion or read together and take collaborative notes on a Google Doc or Google Slide.

These collaborations can happen with or without speaking to each other. In the case of each student contributing their individual work/reflection to a shared document, they aren't really working together but might be gaining insight and inspiration from simply seeing each other's ideas on the document. If they are reading and discussing, you'll want them to be on a Google Meet or group together.

Another benefit to having students collaborate on one document is that it makes it much easier to review and share at the end of class.

Group Work

Breaking up students into small groups to work is vital when hosting synchronous classes online. If you've ever had a video conferencing discussion with more than four people, you know how exhausting and frustrating it is to try to communicate effectively.

Grouping students allows them to unmute their microphones and talk freely. Ideally, groups are no larger than four students, but accommodations may be needed for big classes.

The way you will technically execute group work when teaching synchronously online will depend largely on which video conferencing software you use.

Zoom

Zoom's free and premium versions have the option to split classes into as many as 50 individual "breakout rooms," splitting participants either randomly or manually.

The nice thing about Zoom is you can easily manage where your students go by clicking the "breakout" button to send them to their groups, and "close all breakout rooms" to bring everyone back to the main meeting.

In addition, you can preassign groups, broadcast messages to all groups, and easily navigate between the "rooms" as you check in on your students.

Google Meet

Google Meet now has a breakout room function built into its Google for Education Enterprise edition (a premium product). Their feature allows you to "shuffle" students into random groups or drag and drop them into custom rooms. There are timers and an "I need help" button for students, and it is easy to jump back and forth between rooms as the teacher.

If you don't have access to the Enterprise edition, I devised a system of creating multiple meeting rooms and hyperlinking them into a Google Doc, along with text boxes with the names of the students in each group. I share this document with my students, and from there they navigate to their small-group rooms themselves.

I outline step by step how to do this in a blog post, **"Group Activity over Google Meet**."

Microsoft Teams

Similar to Google Meet, Microsoft has released a feature for breakout rooms where you can have teams "automatically" assign rooms or manually assign them yourself. Some nice features within Teams include the ability to force participants into their rooms and push announcements to all students.

Once my students know how to access the breakout rooms, I make sure expectations are clear before sending students off to do work. Here are a few best practices that I recommend, as shown in Figure 2.15:

1. Designate a "screen sharer." This student will be responsible for sharing their screen as the group works (usually on a collaborative document) so that everyone in the group can see where they are in the assignment. Typically I put a star next to the name of the screen sharer on my slide deck when I am introducing the activity.

2. If you've been in a breakout room with middle or high school students, you probably know how silent and awkward they can get. By providing students with a sentence starter or prompt before you release them to work, the brave student willing to unmute their mic first will know exactly what to say. For example, "Who has an idea on what topic we should select?" or "What were your impressions of the character?"

3. If you are coordinating breakout groups with students who are both in the school building and working remotely, consider how easy/difficult it will be to communicate with the students working remotely from home, and how you could accommodate them to be sure their voices are heard. Sometimes grouping students who are learning remotely with each other is the easiest method for discussion-based activities.

Group Work Best Practices

Designate a screen sharer

Provide sentence stems or prompts to start discussion

Consider volume levels for students in the building

EMPOWERED~edu

Figure 2.15: Best practices for group work.

After students have gotten started, I spend my time bouncing in and out of each room to check their progress, answer questions, support them, and encourage their work. Although it's true that the groups whose rooms I am not in are technically unsupervised for that time, it doesn't actually feel that different from moving around a classroom from group to group. In either environment, you can't hear what all students are saying all the time.

The activities students are doing in their groups are often similar to what I have them do in a classroom: reading, discussing, working through an activity together, or collaborating on a project. The main difference is I am always using some sort of collaborative file (as mentioned previously), so that all the students can access the work together.

Independent Work

Oftentimes the practice or application of a skill is completed through a piece of independent work. If possible, I like to give my students a choice in how or where they complete that work: with teacher support, with peer support, or completely independently. Figure 2.16 shows an idea I first saw from educator Esther Park to help facilitate this.

If entirely remote, I like to give students the option of three different "breakout rooms." However, instead of creating the breakout rooms within the

Meeting Rooms

1 Teacher Help

2 Group Work - talking

3 Individual - quiet

Figure 2.16: Independent work options.

video conferencing platform, I give students a document (most often a Google Slide) with the three rooms represented by three different doors, each linked to a different Google Meeting. The document also contains instructions for the independent work, and instructions for what to do if finished early. When it is time to start I share a link to the document with the students who open it, read their instructions, and navigate to where they'd like to work.

One very useful tool is the **Mute Tab** Chrome extension, which will allow you to open all the breakout rooms in your browser at the same time, then mute/unmute the individual tabs, without having to mute the entire website or hear the chaotic cacophony of all the rooms at once.

Bring it back to the building

In a brick-and-mortar classroom, you can color-coordinate sections of your classroom to match these options. Then, during independent work time, students will need to move (always good!) to the section of the room that they think will best meet their needs. Students who want to work independently have a dedicated space, and students who need help know exactly where to go.

Discussions

Although I love small-group work and I use it for the majority of my synchronous online lessons, there are instances where I really want to have a robust discussion as a whole class.

As an English teacher, Socratic seminars are a regular part of my instruction, and I don't think these types of valuable discussions need to be sacrificed in remote learning. Instead, like most other lessons, they can be adapted using technology and facilitation.

Without firm facilitation an online/video discussion can be chaotic. Students don't have the visual and auditory cues to indicate who might start speaking next, and with video conferencing lag times you often have students talking over each other.

My technique is simply to call on students to unmute their microphones to speak. Although you could have students use the hand-raising feature in their video conferencing platform to determine who to call on, there is a much better tool for facilitating discussion called **Parlay**.

Parlay is an online discussion platform that can be used for asynchronous, chat-room style discussions or live synchronous discussions.

Parlay live discussions provide students with a toolbar with four buttons to click to signal when they feel ready to contribute to the conversation (essentially an advanced virtual hand-raising). They can "tap in" to build on an idea, ask a question, challenge a thought, or introduce a new topic. Once a student "taps in," their avatar moves to the center of the screen and indicates how they'd like to contribute and the amount of times that student has contributed thus far, so the facilitator can easily decide whom to call on next. Once the student is finished speaking or no longer wishes to contribute, they simply click on their toolbar again to "tap out" and the avatar is removed from the center of the screen. This movement in and out of the screen helps the conversation to feel more dynamic, along with icons accompanying each avatar that allow classmates to give confetti or "votes" to hear fellow classmates.

Bring it back to the building

Parlay's live discussion tool would work for classroom discussion as well, but how I've most commonly used it in my brick-and-mortar classroom is as a "silent discussion" tool.

Typically, when conducting Socratic seminars in class, there are too many students for one discussion, so we split into two groups. While one group is in the circle discussing, the other group is using the chatroom style discussion on Parlay to silently make comments and discuss what the first group is saying. Then the groups switch. This way, all the students can be engaging in the discussion throughout the entirety of class, whether they are using their voices or their keyboards.

When using Parlay for online Socratic seminars, I teach my students how to split their screens, so that Parlay takes up half the screen and Google Meet takes the other, because students will still need to be communicating by muting and unmuting their microphones in Google Meet.

Once the conversation is finished Parlay provides the teacher with summary data from the entire conversation, including how many times each student "tapped in" to the conversation, the notes they took during the conversation, and the overall class trends.

I have so far used only the free version of Parlay, which gives users a limited amount of discussions, but there is a premium version as well.

In order to get to the heart of a Socratic seminar, which has minimal teacher involvement, you'll need a plan and some tools. At first, I do this facilitation as a way to model it to the students, and then when they are ready, I allow students to step into a leadership role and facilitate for their peers.

Games

The final addition to the portion of class where I am asking students to apply their learning is through gamification.

I love playing games during class.

See Chapter 4, Apply, Create, Explore, for how I use games in my online synchronous classroom.

Wrap-Up, Exit Tickets, and Goodbye

5–15 minutes

I try to reserve the last bit of class for all the students to come back to the whole-class Google Meet to wrap up, share, reflect, and say goodbye.

If my students have been working on a project, I'll have the "screen sharer" from each group share their screen and briefly present and share what their group worked on. If we played a game, I'll typically review questions that were commonly being missed or sections with which I noticed students struggling. If they worked independently, I'll ask for volunteers to share their work. Really, these are the same types of review most teachers do at the end of any class period.

If there is an exit ticket, I usually ask students just to type a response or reflection into the chat box. I look at those responses as quickly as possible and narrate out loud which students are allowed to sign off because their exit ticket is sufficient.

Often I give a vocabulary word and ask students to use it in an original sentence. This is a quick and easy method for exit tickets that require original answers. However, if you are giving a math equation or other question in which you wouldn't want students waiting to see the right answer in the chat box and copy it exactly, you might consider using a Google Classroom question instead, where you can see the student answers as soon as they submit, all on one page, but they can't necessarily see each other's.

Finally, I ask all my students to say goodbye before they leave class. Personally, it feels a little cold and impersonal to just exit out of a video conference (or walk out of a room), so I let my students either type "goodbye" to the class in the chat box or to unmute and say bye before they leave.

Bring it back to the building

I find that using a digital tool to collect exit tickets rather than collecting slips of paper at the door is far superior. It is much easier to assess whether a student has completed the exit ticket digitally and call out that student's name to be dismissed ("Bye Brian, bye Omar, bye Z, almost Peter"). Then, when most of the class has been dismissed, you are often left with a student or couple of students with whom you need to quickly check in anyway, whether about the content or their executive functioning skills. This method of exit tickets allows you to have that final check-in/sidebar at the end of class before the student leaves for the day.

SYNCHRONOUS INSTRUCTION: KEEP IT FUN

It can be hard to keep students' attention online, especially when they have unlimited games and entertainment at their fingertips and might not have anyone watching to be sure they are dedicating their entire attention to class, so using a few fun tools and techniques for your remote synchronous teaching may help keep students engaged.

Zoom Call Soundboard

Zoom Call Soundboard is a just-for-fun tool, but sometimes those are the ones our students remember and appreciate most.

This tool, contrary to what the name suggests, can be used with any video conferencing software or within the brick-and-mortar classroom, because it is simply a website with different buttons that play audio snippets that might enhance your lessons (see Figure 2.17). The applause button, for example, could be used after students share a piece of work, or the "crickets" button to break the tension when no one is volunteering to speak. You just keep this website open off to the side of your video screen and go to it when a sound effect is just what you need.

Figure 2.17: Zoom Call Soundboard.

Confetti! Confetti All Over . . . What Else?

Confetti is a Chrome extension. Once downloaded and clicked, it will rain confetti all over your screen.

Keep in mind, this is effective only if your screen is the one being shared. But you may choose to use it if you are celebrating birthdays, successes, or sharing student work.

(Remember to refresh your screen before trying it for the first time.)

Uhmmm. . . This Is Awkward

As teachers, we are accustomed to wait time (waiting a decent amount of time after asking a question for students to generate an answer and giving them a chance to volunteer to respond). After a while it doesn't feel awkward to us at all anymore.

However, sometimes that awkward silence can cause students to start panicking, and no one can think clearly when they are panicking.

Uhmmm. . . This Is Awkward. . . is an app that plays elevator music on Zoom, Meet, or any other video conferencing software when too much time has passed without anyone speaking.

It's silly, it's fun.

"Guest Speakers"

During my grammar units, I have "Sargent Pass" (Figure 2.18) come visit our class to guest lecture. Sargent Pass (me in an army green hat and jacket) puts students through the paces as they work through grammar boot camp lesson activities, including digital escape rooms, Pear Deck practice, and random "drills" thrown in where students have to run a lap around the room or do jumping jacks.

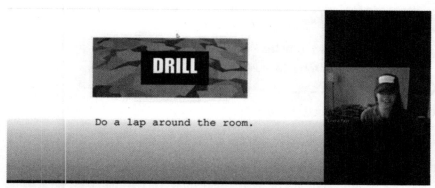

Figure 2.18: Emma Pass as guest speaker "Sargent Pass."

Leah Carper (@how_I_teach_high_school), high school English teacher, transforms into her guest characters during remote teaching by knocking on her desk, telling her students she needs to answer the door, and then she places a sticky note over her camera as she quickly transitions into a costume. She narrates the conversation between herself and this guest speaker as she is transitioning, and when she removes the sticky note, voila! **Grammar Grandma** or **Detective Context** are there to give a lesson to the class.

Music

I love playing music before class or during independent work time. As I mention in Chapter 9, Building Culture and Community, I often ask students to submit on a Google Form music they like to listen to, and I use those responses to create a custom playlist. You might even ask your students which of their classmates chose each song to see how well they know each other.

Bring it back to the building

All of these tools and strategies can easily be brought back to the brick-and-mortar classroom.

Here are a few great (school appropriate) playlists I've found when I want to set the tone myself:

- **Clean Chillhop** on Spotify
- Classroom Appropriate Music by **@missbensko** on Spotify
- **Top 100 Clean Classroom Playlist** on YouTube

RESOURCES

Items in **bold** in the text are listed here in the Resources. Direct access to all the following resources is available at **https://hybridteacherresource.com** and on this book's page on www.wiley.com.

Zoom—https://zoom.us

Microsoft Teams—https://www.microsoft.com/en-us/microsoft-365/microsoft-teams

Google Meet—https://meet.google.com

Backchannel Chat—https://backchannelchat.com

Google Jamboard—https://jamboard.google.com

Microsoft Whiteboard—https://apps.apple.com/us/app/microsoft-whiteboard/id1352499399

Zoom Whiteboard—https://support.zoom.us/hc/en-us/articles/205677665-Sharing-a-whiteboard

Whiteboard.fi—https://whiteboard.fi

Classroom Screen—https://classroomscreen.com

GoNoodle—https://www.gonoodle.com

SuperMovers—https://www.bbc.co.uk/teach/supermovers

Mari Venturino's Twitter: https://twitter.com/MsVenturino

Move It Chrome Extension—https://chrome.google.com/webstore/detail/move-it/kopilngnmfklhhjocdfdlokmodibcbmk

Google Slides—https://www.google.com/slides/about/

Pear Deck—https://www.peardeck.com

Pear Deck Introductory Tutorial—https://www.youtube.com/watch?v=rj9Bs-FDaHs

Nearpod—https://nearpod.com/login

Class Kick—https://classkick.com

William Beeland Study—https://vtext.valdosta.edu/xmlui/bitstream/handle/10428/1252/beeland_am.pdf?sequence=1&isAllowed=y

Custom Cursor for Chrome—https://chrome.google.com/webstore/detail/custom-cursor-for-chrome/ogdlpmhglpejoiomcodnpjnfgcpmgale

Online-Stopwatch—https://www.online-stopwatch.com/classroom-timers/

Google Version History—https://support.google.com/docs/answer/190843?co=GENIE.Platform%3DDesktop&hl=en

Progressive Stories via Google Docs—https://www.edtechemma.com/single-post/2020/05/14/Progressive-Stories-via-Google-Docs

Google Meet—https://meet.google.com

Group Activity over Google Meet—https://www.edtechemma.com/single-post/2020/03/26/group-activity-over-google-meet

Mute Tab—https://chrome.google.com/webstore/detail/mute-tab/blljobffcekcbopmkgfhpcjmbfnelkfg

Parlay—https://parlayideas.com

Zoom Call Soundboard—https://view.ceros.com/editorial-content/soundboard/p/1

Confetti—https://chrome.google.com/webstore/detail/confetti-confetti-allove/alnpfmeemhhcfephffidoflphgnneeld/related

Uhmmm… This Is Awkward…—https://uhmmm.app

Grammar Grandma or Detective Context—https://www.tiktok.com/@how_i_teach_high_school/video/6880577923124923654?lang=en

Clean Chill Hop—https://open.spotify.com/playlist/6SYSh1qeZj TomYu0Drwmis

Classroom Appropriate Music by @missbensko—https://open.spotify.com/ search/%40missbensko

Top 100 Clean Classroom Playlist—https://www.youtube.com/watch?v=AqA JLh9wuZ0&list=PLpXA1IqBgeZROfhsGkUE2HrFGN7bKqgpF

Chapter 3
Asynchronous Learning

The greatest sign of success for a teacher is to be able to say, "The children are now working as if I did not exist."

—*Maria Montessori*

Asynchronous Learning
Students access learning at different times and work through it at their own pace.

How often do all students need the exact same amount of time to complete a task? If you are a teacher, you know the answer is never. Which is why asynchronous learning is one of the major advantages to a hybrid school system.

Allowing students the freedom and agency to work through something on their own timeline can relieve stress for some and prevent boredom-based, attention-seeking behavior from others.

Even better, asynchronous learning doesn't have to be limited to online or hybrid educational models. I've used asynchronous learning in my traditional brick-and-mortar classroom too.

Bring it back to the building

When I taught 6th-grade English in Las Vegas, I dedicated two days/week to asynchronous learning, where the students had access to their "student-directed lessons" on Google Classroom and knew on those days they could choose where to work, who to work with, and direct the entire experience.

On those days I would project onto the front of the room "Student-Directed Learning Day" and students would come into class, see that notification, and immediately choose their seats and go to Google Classroom to access their work. Because we did this several days a week, there were typically a couple of assignments to choose from and students could complete those in any order. I tried to give students a lot of independence on these days, and they knew that if they chose to socialize or goof around for part of class, the expectation was that they would need to finish their work at home. For eager students who could finish their asynchronous work quickly, they knew they always had the option for "academic free time" (reading, writing, drawing, educational games) or they could access a number of extension activities in a separate Google Classroom I had created called "English Beyond." Every quarter I would check these extension activities and put student names into a hat for every extension activity they completed. Then I would draw a number of prizes, raffle style, as a way to positively reinforce finishing asynchronous work early and choosing to do extension activities.

While students worked on their asynchronous lessons, I monitored the classroom, answered questions, and most important could help higher-need students individually or in small groups.

In addition, asynchronous learning requires students to develop important executive functioning skills, which will not only help them succeed in school but in their future careers as well (see more on this in Chapter 7, Executive Functioning Skills).

Is asynchronous learning the answer to all of our institutional/educational problems? Of course not; there are downsides to asynchronous learning too. Some students rush through the work in order to have more free time in their day, so they will need to be encouraged to work more slowly and dig deeper. Other students will take much more time than necessary and will need to be encouraged to prioritize and manage their time.

You will quickly understand which students are which, especially if you include meta-learning reflections with your assignments ("Did you spend more or less time than my prediction? What percentage of time did you spend on XYZ?")

During synchronous learning days, I typically dedicate a portion of time to checking in with those student groups and making sure they are getting the support they need.

At PSD Global Academy (PGA) Middle School our learning schedule looks like this:

Monday	Tuesday	Wednesday	Thursday	Friday
Asynchronous	Synchronous	Asynchronous	Synchronous	Asynchronous
Lessons typically support prior learning or ongoing projects.	*Check-in with students about Friday's/Monday's asynchronous lessons.* *Introduce new content.*	*Lessons typically support content from Tuesday's synchronous lesson.*	*Check in with students about Wednesday's asynchronous lessons.* *Introduce new content.*	*Lessons typically support content from Thursday's synchronous lesson.*

I think it is critically important to take time to check in with students about their asynchronous learning on your in-person days so that student work is held to a high standard.

At PGA we build this into the schedule in a few ways. Math and language arts both have an extra hour of time built into our in-person synchronous learning days called "What I Need" (WIN) hours. I'll often use WIN time to split students into groups based on their needs from their previous asynchronous learning. We also have students come to campus on Wednesdays for "open lab" where they have the opportunity to work on their asynchronous work independently or with peers, and teachers can check in with individuals or groups of students as needed.

In short, make sure your asynchronous work is meaningful and make sure your students know that.

ACCESSING ASYNCHRONOUS LEARNING: LEARNING MANAGEMENT SYSTEMS (LMS)

Once you've established your schedule, the next thing to determine is how your students will access their asynchronous work.

Schools and districts have been handling this in a number of ways based on the access they and their students have to technology, ranging from paper-packet pickup, to email, to learning management systems. This might surprise you, but I don't think there is a bad system as long as it works for students. (In the section "Access to Technology" in Chapter 14, I'll discuss some more ideas on delivery for students with limited access to technology.)

If most students do have reliable access to a device and internet, by far the easiest method for both delivering and collecting asynchronous learning is through a learning management system (LMS).

Learning management systems have been designed to post work, communicate with students, give feedback, and grade easily and efficiently all within the same platform. Think of them as very interactive websites customized for your class.

As was true when I discussed video conferencing software, there are plenty of LMS options to choose from. For the sake of simplicity I have chosen to highlight three of the most popular LMS options: **Google Classroom, Schoology,** and **Canvas**. I have taught with all of these to some extent, and also gathered some input from other teachers to compile these pro/con lists:

Google Classroom

Pros	Cons
• Free	• Not all district gradebooks integrate with Google Classroom's gradebook
• Intuitive	
• Post to individual or student groups	• No folders or subfolders
• Integration with Google Drive and YouTube	• No attendance records built in
• Google Meet integration	
• Student "mute" feature	
• Grading window with scrolling feature and comment bank	
• Guardian summaries of student work	

Schoology

Pros	Cons
• Built-in assessment tools	• Cost
• Save questions for future use	• Classroom discussions are not intuitive
• Attendance record	
• Folders and subfolders	• Outdated design
• "Turn It In" plagiarism checker integration	• Navigation and settings aren't always intuitive
• Time limit options	
• Parent codes	
• **Badges**!	

Canvas

Pros	Cons
• Personalize pages for "branded" look	• Cost
• Collaborative documents for group work	• Discussion board doesn't always work properly
• More features for organizing work	• Not as intuitive or user friendly
• Lesson sharing platform "Canvas Commons"	

I use Google Classroom, not only because it is free but because I find it to be the most user friendly and intuitive to use. Plus, there is an enormous community of Google Educators who are willing and excited to share how to use it and what they are doing in their classrooms. Read more about how to find these resources in Chapter 18, Going Further....

Regardless of the LMS you've chosen, the following sections cover some universal best practices I would recommend.

Post Everything

Post everything you do on your LMS, whether it is synchronous, asynchronous, in person, or online.

I call Google Classroom my "mission control center." Whether my students are doing a full asynchronous lesson, a short in-class activity, going to another site like Khan or Newsela, or even just reading their book for 30 minutes, I post an assignment for it on Google Classroom.

I don't grade all of these assignments, but I like to have a record of everything we do in class. This is especially helpful for students who are absent and can easily check Google Classroom to make up both synchronous and asynchronous work without even needing to talk to me about it.

Stay Organized

The difficulty students experience in finding asynchronous work is one of the greatest barriers to success for online and hybrid learners. Good, consistent organization is an easy way to remove that barrier.

If possible, talk with your grade level or department and make a plan to organize your LMS classes in a consistent way. Then students don't need to know the organizational style of each teacher, because each LMS or course will look the same.

At PGA middle school we organize our Google Classrooms with three header or "topic" types.

- Week at a glance—this is at the very top of the "Classwork" section and only has one document (or "material") under it, updated each week to give students an overview of the week's learning targets, lessons, and assignments so that students can update their planners at the start of each week, or get in touch with teachers about upcoming assignments or events. (Figure 3.1)

Week at a Glance 👀

Figure 3.1: Week at a glance.

- Week #—Then there are a series of headers, each with a week number. The current week is always closest to the top and all the assignments for that week are posted there.
- Class Materials—At the bottom is a section for ongoing or miscellaneous items. I have my class syllabus, resources for accessing digital books, and class surveys posted in this section.

Then we label or title the assignments in a specific way, starting with a number, corresponding to the current week, followed by a letter that represents the day of the week that assignment should be completed. Next we label it by the type of assignment it is and finally the name of the assignment. (Figure 3.2)

→ Week 16

📋 16M - Assignment - Peer Feedback	Due Dec 7
📋 16M - Independent Reading - Reading Log	Due Dec 7
🔲 16TU - In-Class - Hero's Game Plan	Posted Dec 8
📋 16W - Independent Reading	Due Dec 9
📋 16F- Catch-Up Friday - Language Arts	Due Dec 11

Figure 3.2: Assignment labels.

Although this might seem like a lot of detail to put into an assignment title, it really helps when searching for work (with a number + letter combo, simply use the "CTRL" and "F" buttons on your keyboard to search for the assignment and it will come up right away), or when teaching your students how to prioritize completing missing assignments (start with bigger pieces of work labeled "assignments" and "assessment" before smaller pieces of work labeled "do now").

Within the assignment directions we always start with an estimate on the amount of time the work should take, so that students can set timers and plan their schedule. Then, a set of *simple* instructions. Last, but not least, we include what we call a "learning coach check." Learning coaches are what we call our parents and guardians, and this is a simple directive to help them understand if their student has done the work or not. We are not asking them to assess the work or give feedback, simply hold their student accountable for getting their work done each day (Figure 3.3).

 13F - Assignment - Constructed Response

Posted Nov 20

🕐 Time: 25-35 mins

👀 Instructions:
1. Follow the instructions on the attached Doc, including watching the video, answering the questions, and constructing your response.
2. Turn in.

📌 LC Check: Open the attached Doc and make sure there is a paragraph of text.

R.A.C.E - The Hobbit
Google Docs

Figure 3.3: Learning coach check.

Create Spaces for Socialization

Every LMS typically has a space for general announcements and communications; it's called "Home" in Schoology and "Stream" in Google Classroom. When students aren't able to come to the brick-and-mortar building every day they are also losing precious social-emotional learning time.

Because students don't have their lunchrooms or hallways to socialize in, I not only allow but encourage students to socialize on my Google Classroom Stream.

Each morning, on asynchronous learning days, I'll post a simple announcement to the stream saying "Hello," detailing the work for that day, and then I'll post a "community question" and encourage students to answer it in the chat box shown in Figure 3.4.

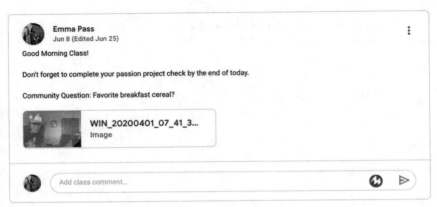

Figure 3.4: Community question with answer box.

Recently, I've also been posting selfies with my morning messages, in order to remind the students I am always there to support them, even if they can't always see me. It was a little awkward at first, but I found posing with pets, hats, and even houseplants helped.

I'll also post various questions, memes, and videos to the stream throughout the week and encourage students to do the same.

My philosophy is, if the students are motivated to log on to see the meme, or participate in the social chat, they are one step closer to doing their work.

I also check in with the Stream from time to time during the day, commenting on students' posts to remind them of my presence, and encourage any students who might have been on there a little too long to refocus on their schoolwork.

If you are reading this thinking, "No way could my students handle this! It would be bananas," I would encourage you to start the year with a conversation about communication online and digital footprints. Try to teach your students how to use online spaces responsibly. Then, if that doesn't work, Google Classroom (and I assume most LMS) have settings for **limiting who is able to post**.

Use Text and Icons

Although graphics and visual appeal might not increase student comprehension, students tend to prefer work that looks visually engaging, increasing their odds of actually completing that piece of work or using that virtual space.

In the case of an LMS, Google Classroom for example, you can use different text and icons to make your classroom stand out. For example, emojis can be used anywhere there is a text field, so consider using emojis in your headers ("topics") or in your assignment instructions to make key elements pop.

If you want to take it a step further, you can use a website like **Cool Symbol**'s fancy font changer, to copy/paste custom fonts into your topic and headers or assignments (See Figure 3.5).

Figure 3.5: Google Classroom topic using Cool Symbol.

DESIGNING ASYNCHRONOUS LESSONS

Once you've become familiar with your LMS, the work truly begins. It's time to design your asynchronous instruction.

Typically, when I am designing an asynchronous lesson for my students, I want to include the following:

- The learning target
- An overview of the lesson
- Direct instruction (video or audio)
- Written assignment instructions
- Links to further practice, application, or assessment
- Class communication or collaboration
- Reflection

If you are using an LMS like Canvas or Schoology, you could build these components right into the platform. However, with Google Classroom as my LMS, I build asynchronous lessons within a Google Slide deck.

There are plenty of reasons why I prefer a Google Slide deck to a Google Doc or Word Doc when creating these lessons. First, Google Slides are easy to make visually engaging through slide templates (**SlidesGo**), and they are easier to manipulate as a graphic design tool. Also, content is naturally chunked into pieces in a slide deck, which reduces cognitive overload (see Chapter 5, Keep Design in Mind, for more on this). Finally, Slides can be used not only to deliver instructions but to collect student responses, like you might with a worksheet. As long as each student has their own copy of the slide deck (easily done in Google Classroom by selecting "make a copy" on the file or **"forcing" a copy when sharing the link**), you'll be able to deliver and collect information all within the same deck.

The following is an example of what an asynchronous lesson might look like in Google Slides. The images have been taken from an asynchronous **slide deck template** that you can view in its entirety or "make a copy" of to reuse for your own lessons.

Step 1: Title, Text, Overview

The first three slides in my lesson are simple enough: an engaging title slide, a learning target, and an overview of the lesson (see Figure 3.6).

Figure 3.6: My first three slides in my lessons.

I like to include an overview based on feedback from students who like to know where the lesson is going and how involved it is going to be before they begin.

Step 2: Direct Instruction Video

Then, I almost always include a video (see Figure 3.7).
There are lots of different ways to find or film a video.

- **Screen Record**

    When I have time, I screen record my own videos. I use a tool called **Screencastify** that allows me to record quickly and easily through the help of their Chrome Extension. Once it's installed, it can sit in the

Figure 3.7: A video is included.

top right corner of your Chrome browser and you can begin recording in seconds.

When you start recording, you can either record your entire computer screen (so students can see your lesson slides or demonstration), just your face (good for recording an announcement), or a little of both. When you are sharing your screen and your webcam is enabled, your face appears as a little box in the bottom corner. As you can see in Figure 3.7, this is typically the setting I go for.

Once I start the recording, I'm usually "presenting" a Google Slide deck on my screen and delivering a lesson or reviewing content. I'll also ask questions and leave brief pauses to allow for student response via Edpuzzle or Google Slides (more on this later in this section).

When I've finished the lesson, I'll demonstrate the activity I want my students to do for the remainder of their asynchronous work. If the activity is posted on Google Classroom, I'll go to Google Classroom and show the students exactly where to go to access the rest of their work. If the work is attached in a Google Slide deck, I'll go to the Google Slide deck and demonstrate exactly what to do there. Students should have no questions about where and how to access the rest of the work (as long as they watched the video).

One nice feature about Screencastify is that it saves your video directly to your Google Drive. Then, within Google Slides you can simply click "insert," "video," and select your recently recorded Screencastify directly from the Drive tab. There is no need to download or upload the video, and it only takes seconds from the moment you finish recording to having the video uploaded to your slides.

Because filming and adding videos to Google Slides is so quick and easy, I typically record multiple videos per lesson. I've found that the shorter the video, the more likely students are to watch it, so I prefer to film several 1–2 minute videos rather than one 10-minute video.

- **YouTube**

Although screen recording is my go-to tool, as I've said in earlier chapters, sometimes you have to work smarter and not harder. If you are teaching something based on the common-core state standards, chances are there is a teacher that has already posted a lesson on YouTube.

Sometimes reinventing the wheel is not the answer. Feel no shame in using YouTube.

YouTube videos can also be inserted directly into your Google Slide deck by clicking "insert," "video," and either copying/pasting your URL into that window, or searching for it directly within YouTube (see Figure 3.8).

Once you have a video, there are a couple of different ways for your students to engage with it.

One issue I've run into is that after I've put all my care and effort into making (or finding) a video for my students, some of them just skip it and decide not to watch.

To be fair, I don't always love watching instructional videos, especially if they are longer than about a minute (remember, TikTok videos are typically between 5 and 60 seconds long), which is why it is so important to require student engagement with your videos. Here are several options for that:

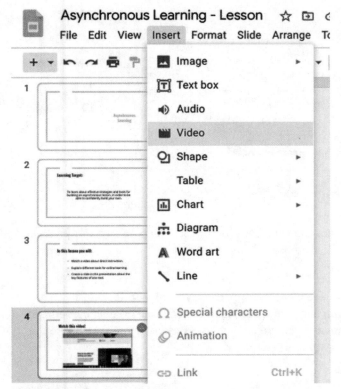

Figure 3.8: Inserting video into a Google Slide Deck.

- **Video Formatting on Google Slides**

  Earlier I mentioned that I ask students to answer questions during my prerecorded lessons. One way to capture those student answers is by adding a text box to the Google slide alongside your video and have your students add their answer there.

  Then, with your video highlighted, click "video formatting" and on the right-hand side you'll see an editing column that will allow you to determine when you'd like the video to automatically start and end (Figure 3.9).

  If your first question is at one minute, set the video to start at 0:00 and end at 1:00. Next, duplicate that slide and set the video on your second slide to start at 1:00 and end at your next question.

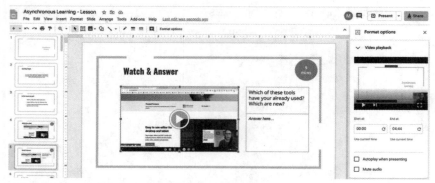

Figure 3.9: Formatting video start and end.

This way you are chunking your content and keeping students engaged by asking simple comprehension questions.

- **Edpuzzle**

  If you like the idea of video formatting, you might take it up a notch. Instead of inserting your video into a slide deck, you could upload it to a site like **Edpuzzle** (Figure 3.10) or **PlayPosit** and include a link in the slides for your students to follow.

Figure 3.10: Edpuzzle video editing.

Sites like Edpuzzle allow you to embed those interactive questions directly into the videos, so the video will pause at the question and only restart once it's been answered. The benefit of using a site like this is it will also track your students on the back end, so you can see which students accessed the video, for how long, and their individual answers. The programs can auto-grade multiple-choice questions, giving students immediate feedback on their responses. (Go to the Edpuzzle website for a short tutorial on how Edpuzzle works.)

Which to use?

Between Screencastify, YouTube, Edpuzzle, and Google Slide Video Formatting, it might seem like a little much. I suggest starting with one strategy and mastering it (YouTube and Google Slides Formatting, perhaps) then coming back to these instructions and trying the rest.

I use a combination of all of the above in my asynchronous lessons. If what I am trying to teach is really content heavy, I'll record my own videos and upload them to Edpuzzle. If it is mostly review/instructional, I'll use YouTube and Video Formatting to keep it simple.

Step 3: Assignment Directions

Even if I've gone over the directions for the activity in a video, I also like to summarize them in text as well, as shown in Figure 3.11. If a student needs to review the instructions, they are more likely to go back to the written text than find the spot in the video where you are explaining a certain step.

You'll also notice I added a time bubble in the top right corner; this links to a countdown timer. Not all students will choose to use it, and not all of them need to, but some students benefit from timers to help them manage their time on a remote learning day.

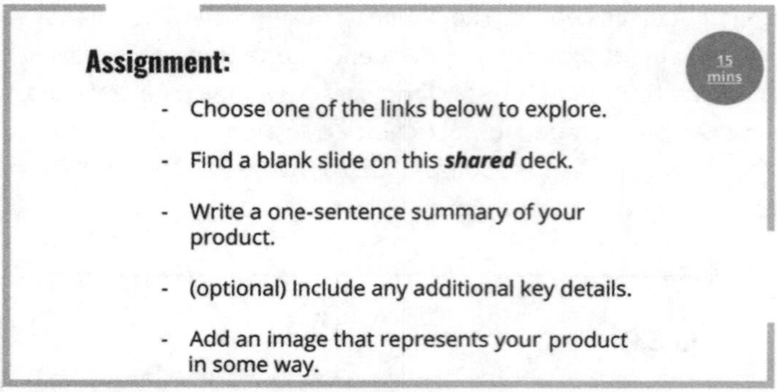

Assignment:

- Choose one of the links below to explore.

- Find a blank slide on this *shared* deck.

- Write a one-sentence summary of your product.

- (optional) Include any additional key details.

- Add an image that represents your product in some way.

15 mins

Figure 3.11: Assignment instructions.

Step 4: Apply, Create, Explore

The bulk of any asynchronous lesson is having students use the content knowledge to create, practice, play, explore, or assess. There are endless ways to do this.

Sometimes the students are tasked to do something non-tech-related (i.e. draw a poster, create a sculpture/structure, make a recipe, find something in nature/outside, etc.) In this example, I ask them to take a photo and add it to their Slide assignment.

Other times, students are going to another website to complete their work. See Chapter 4, Apply, Create, Explore, for examples and EdTech tools I like to use here. Figure 3.12 demonstrates a choice board activity I use in professional development with teachers to explore some of these tools.

If students are creating as a part of the activity, I'll typically leave a place in the Google Slide assignment for them to copy/paste a link to their creation as shown in Figure 3.13, or a space to upload a screenshot or photo they've taken.

Step 5: Connect and Communicate

Some of my favorite EdTech tools allow students to interact with each other, such as **Flipgrid** and **Padlet**. The ability to continue to connect with peers, even when working on remote asynchronous lessons, can help keep students engaged.

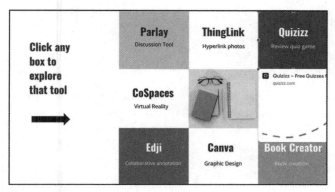

Figure 3.12: Choice board activity.

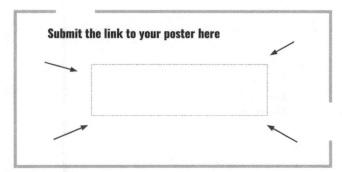

Figure 3.13: Identifying where to paste a link.

If the lesson does not include a peer-to-peer interaction, I try to encourage students to still connect with each other as a part of a sharing or reflection in the lesson (see Figure 3.14).

Step 6: Reflection

I like to end each lesson with a quick reflection. Sometimes that is a comprehension question on the subject (like an exit ticket), or sometimes it is a meta-learning reflection.

Metacognition is the process of thinking about our thinking, and research shows that meta-learning techniques can be beneficial to the learning process and promote the development of executive functioning skills. In fact, a study conducted by **Katherine Larson and Michael Gerber** found that, "For learning

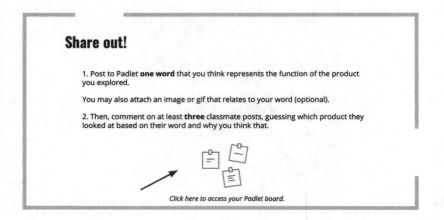

Figure 3.14: Encourage students to connect with each other.

disabled and low achieving students, metacognitive training can improve behavior more effectively than traditional attention control training," and according to another study by **Mary-Ann Winkelmes**, "It has even been shown to increase academic self-confidence of non-Caucasian students in the STEM disciplines."

To incorporate metacognition techniques into your lesson reflections, Maya Bialik, who holds a master's degree in Mind, Brain & Education from Harvard, suggests using questions like:

- Do you know more, a lot more, or no more about this topic now vs when you started?
- Approximately how much time did you spend on this assignment?
- When you look at your score, what caused you to lose points?
- Did this assignment take you as much, less, or more time than you thought it would?
- What was the most difficult part of this assignment for you?
- What did you enjoy about this assignment?
- What would you do differently if you were to design it?
- What questions do you still have?

Even if students don't have an answer for every question every time, the process of reflecting is a good habit at the end of any project or assignment.

These reflections could be done on a Google Slide with a text box for responses or linked to a short Google Form survey.

Step 7: Turn In

Finally, the last slide in my asynchronous lesson is always a reminder to "turn in" or "mark as done" their work in Google Classroom. This is in an attempt to help students develop organizational skills in their LMS.

I also add a fun gif to celebrate the completion of the work (Figure 3.15).

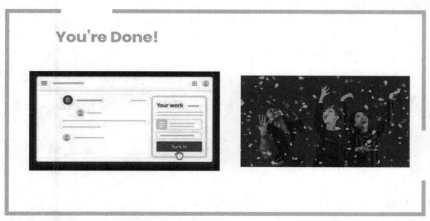

Figure 3.15: Celebrate the completion of the work.

Examples

If you are anything like me, good examples are the best way to understand how a finished product might look. The following sections provide a couple of examples of asynchronous lessons I have used in my class.

Grammar Bootcamp

Grammar Bootcamp was conducted as a follow-up to a virtual "obstacle course" we complete in class. In the lesson I review the activities and then ask students to practice the concepts on Khan Academy.

Figure 3.16 shows title, learning target, and overview.

Figure 3.16: Title, learning target, and overview.

In this lesson, instead of a postsurvey or reflection, I ask students to complete a presurvey where they assess their current understanding of grammar concepts we would be learning that year.

Then the students view a series of short (less than three minute) videos explaining the "obstacle course" activities, plus answer comprehension/video check questions within the slides. (See Figure 3.17.)

Figure 3.17: Short videos explaining the "obstacle course" activities, plus comprehension/video check questions.

Then, I include a link to Khan Academy with our class code. Activities have already been assigned to students there.

Finally, a slide reminding students to turn their work in on Google Classroom. (See Figure 3.18.)

Figure 3.18: Reminding students to turn in their work.

Vocabulary

This is a lesson that I repeatedly give to students throughout the year, whenever there is vocabulary that should be pretaught before a piece of text or video.

I use a **template** of the lesson structure and make a copy of it every time I need to teach vocabulary. (Use the Make a Copy command from the File menu.)

Figure 3.19 shows the lesson title, learning target, overview.

Figure 3.19: Lesson title, learning target, verview.

Figure 3.20 shows the instructions to join Quizlet, create a new deck (or open an existing one), and the words I want students to use in their vocabulary deck.

Figure 3.20: Instructions to join Quizlet, create a new deck, and words to use in their vocabulary deck.

Figure 3.21 shows the instructions to use their new words on Quizlet to play a review game and paste a screenshot of their top score on the Google Slide deck.

Then, students select seven vocab words and write synonyms for each.

Finally, students choose seven vocab words and use them in an original sentence.

Figure 3.21: Instructions for playing a review game and pasting a screenshot of their top score.

A "You're Done" slide (shown in Figure 3.22) reminds students to turn in their work on Google Classroom.

Figure 3.22: "You're Done" slide.

ASYNCHRONOUS DISCUSSION

As I mentioned previously, incorporating discussion in asynchronous/remote learning not only helps develop discussion skills but also supports your class community.

There are several great tools to facilitate asynchronous discussion:

- **Google Classroom Question**—Allows teachers to post a question and (optional) materials. Students leave short answer responses in a text box. The teacher must enable the "Students can reply to each other" check box when setting up the question to allow students to post responses to one another's work (only after they have submitted their own).

- **LMS Discussion Boards—Canvas**—Similar to a Google Classroom question with the distinction of being able to create a "focused discussion," which are typically shorter interactions with one layer of posting and one layer of commenting. Alternatively, you can create a "threaded discussion," which has an unlimited amount of comment nesting, meaning the discussions can be longer and more complex.

- **LMS Discussion Boards—Schoology**—Similar to a Google Classroom question, the benefit to Schoology's discussion board is the ability to select an individual student and see the number of times they have contributed to the discussion, which will make assessing each student much easier!

- **Flipgrid**—Video-based discussion tool. Teachers can post a video or text-based prompt as well as other file types, and students submit their responses via a short video recording. The default setting posts the student's Flipgrid video response onto the class board for other students to watch and respond to either by video or text.

- **Padlet**—A collaborative class board where students can post responses via text, gif, video, image, or audio. Responses can be formatted to show up in a "cork board" style or many other formats.

- **Parlay**—Has already been discussed for its synchronous discussion tools but can also be used for asynchronous discussions in a text-based discussion. Some benefits to using Parlay include the ability to make students anonymous to one another, a prompt for sentence stems, and the "Parlay Universe," where teachers can search for prebuilt lessons and discussion prompts to use in their own classrooms.

Each of these tools will give students the opportunity to post and for classmates to respond.

But simply providing your students the instruction to "respond" to their peers will probably not yield the high-quality and robust discussion you are looking for.

I get a lot of "I agree" or "That's good," when my students respond to each other without instruction.

In her article, **"Making Online Discussions Meaningful,"** Virtual Learning director **Elaine Plybon** proposes teaching specific models for sharing and giving feedback that will provide the structure students need to construct meaningful responses.

Here a few protocols that Plybon recommends:

The Final Word	After reading a text, students post a single word or short quote from the text that they think represents its greater meaning.
	Then, all students are instructed to respond to their peers by guessing why that word or phrase was chosen.
	Finally, the original student gets to respond to their own post to clarify their intent.
What If?	Students are instructed to respond with "What if. . . ?" or "Yes, but. . ." to their classmates' original posts.
The Four A's	Students are split into two groups, "agree" and "argue."
	After engaging with a text, they will need to respond to the text by either agreeing with it or arguing against it.
	Then, the students are instructed to respond to two students' posts in the opposing group, making a case for their side using evidence from the text.

OTHER ASYNCHRONOUS OPTIONS

Although the **Google Slide example** described in this section is the most common way I design an asynchronous lesson, it certainly isn't the only way. Here are a couple of other options you might consider for developing asynchronous instruction:

- **Pear Deck**

  As you may recall, **Pear Deck** is one of my favorite EdTech tools. The ability to directly add interactive questions (multiple choice, short answer, etc.) into Google Slides (or PowerPoint) makes it easy to collect formative assessment data while delivering a lesson synchronously. There is also an option to make the lesson "self-paced" so students can move through the lesson independently and interact with the materials, follow links, and answer questions, just like you might have them do in Google Slides.

One of the benefits of using Pear Deck is that students won't be able to edit any of the original slide material within Pear Deck; they can only manipulate the interactive features you've built in. Plus, Pear Deck has the additional options to draw on slides and embed websites directly into slides, both of which are difficult to accomplish without including a hyperlink.

Pear Deck has also recently added the option to record audio files on individual slides, which is great for giving directions.

The only reason I use Google Slides over Pear Deck for asynchronous lessons is that it is easier for me to grade and give feedback for a Google Slide deck in the Google Classroom grading window than it is for me to grade and give feedback in Pear Deck.

- **HyperDocs**

Some might consider the Google Slides lesson I described previously a "HyperDoc." **HyperDoc**, however, is a trademarked term used to describe a specific template that incorporates hyperlinks in order to extend learning beyond what is possible on pen and paper.

Teachers often use a Google Doc with tables, images, and background colors to create visually appealing, exploratory experiences (see Figure 3.23).

One of the great things about HyperDocs is that there are lots of **free templates** available on the web for you to copy, adapt, and reuse for your own class.

They also follow an **effective framework for designing lessons** (engage, explore, explain, apply, share, reflect, extend) that can be useful to use as a model as you start creating your own asynchronous instruction.

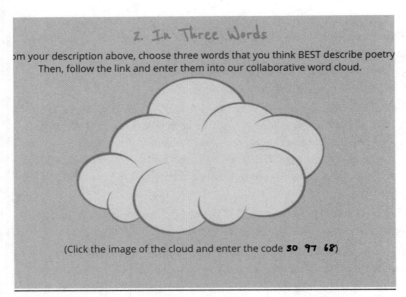

Figure 3.23: Poetry HyperDoc example.

- **Choice Boards**

    Choice is a big word in education at the moment, and for good reason. Choice is powerful in fostering student agency, independence, and engagement. According to Peter Johnston in his book, *Choice Words: How Our Language Affects Children's Learning*, "Students with a strong sense of personal integrity, efficacy, and agency do the following:

- Work harder.
- They have greater focus.
- They have more interest.
- They are less likely to give up.
- They are better at planning.
- They are more likely to choose challenging tasks.
- They set higher goals.
- They have improved concentration when difficulties are faced.
- And the process is iterative, that is, it creates a positive cycle of success."

    One way to foster an additional sense of student agency within asynchronous learning is to create "choice boards" for students in the application/creation stage of learning to empower students to take their learning and apply it in a way that feels the most interesting or meaningful to them.

In my experience, there is a sweet spot for providing choice. Two to three options are usually enough. When you give students a laundry list of choices, they can get overwhelmed.

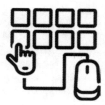

When creating choice boards, another thing to consider is student access to technology and media literacy. You might provide some options that require less and some options that require more technology, so that all students feel like they have the option to choose what works best for them (see Figures 3.24 and 3.25). This is a good practice not only in instances where students might have limited access to technology but also for students who might not have the skills required to work within a certain platform or simply prefer not to work on their computers all day.

Book Cover	Slide Presentation	Book Trailer
Draw a book cover that represents the mood of your novel through symbol and color.	Create a slide deck with at least 5 images and descriptions from your novel that depict the mood.	Make a book trailer video for your book that depicts the mood through imagery and music.

Figure 3.24: Options with higher technology requirements.

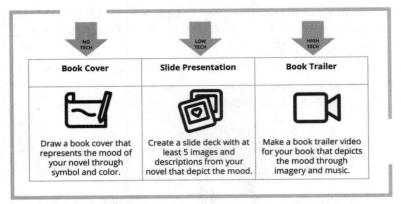

Figure 3.25: Options with lower technology requirements.

MEANINGFUL OR MANDATORY?

Kate Stevens is a language arts educator who wears many hats at PGA, with 10 years of experience in hybrid teaching and learning. She has also designed and coordinated instructional coaching internationally and locally, leading professional development in blended and hybrid pedagogy. In 2015, Kate was recognized with the Colorado Department of Education's Blended & Online Teacher of the Year award.

Kate offers this question to teachers: "Is the work you are posting content rich and educationally valuable for your students? Or are you posting it simply because you feel like you need to have something for the students to do that day?"

If your answer is the latter, she suggests giving students more unstructured, exploratory learning time. Allow students to engage in learning that feels meaningful for them.

But Kate doesn't simply tell her students to have unstructured learning time; she teaches them different methods for doing it. She guides them in identifying personal learning goals and how to use their resources to pursue those needs. When students learn to select a learning target, or design their own, they take on greater ownership of their learning. Then, teaching reflection structures helps students select or design learning targets that not only (i) meet their academic needs but (ii) enhance student engagement.

The next time you find yourself up late scrambling to throw a lesson together, consider that it might be more meaningful to ask your students to create their own learning experience that next day, rather than giving them something you scrambled to purchase on Teachers Pay Teachers that you don't stand fully behind. (*There are plenty of wonderful, meaningful materials on TPT too.*)

RESOURCES

Items in **bold** in the text are listed here in the Resources. Direct access to all the following resources is available at **https://hybridteacherresource.com** and on this book's page on www.wiley.com.

Google Classroom—https://classroom.google.com/u/0/h

Schoology—https://www.schoology.com

Canvas—https://www.canvas.net/

Badges—https://support.schoology.com/hc/en-us/articles/201001833-How-do-I-use-Badges-

Set student permissions to post and comment—https://support.google.com/edu/classroom/answer/6099424?co=GENIE.Platform%3DDesktop&hl=en

Cool Symbol—https://coolsymbol.com/cool-fancy-text-generator.html

SlidesGo—https://slidesgo.com

Force Users to Make a Copy of a Google Doc!—https://shakeuplearning.com/blog/force-users-to-make-a-copy-of-a-google-doc/#:~:text=Open%20the%20doc%2C%20slide%20deck,word%20COPY%20in%20the%20link

Slide Deck Template—https://docs.google.com/presentation/d/1ceUmZmd4x76bJnv4T6E6SISonuU3yU-3vzDpUN_lye8/edit?usp=sharing

Screencastify—https://www.screencastify.com

Edpuzzle—https://edpuzzle.com

Edpuzzle Tutorial—https://edpuzzle.com/media/5ea2f95bfd15 753f09cdc809

FlipGrid—https://info.flipgrid.com

Padlet—https://padlet.com/dashboard

Larson, K. and Gerber, M. (1987). Effects of social metacognitive training for enhancing overt behavior in learning disabled and low achieving delinquents. *Exceptional Children* 54: 201–211. 10.1177/001440298705400302.

Winkelmes, M. (2013, Spring). Transparency in teaching: Faculty share data and improve students' learning. *Liberal Education* 99(2): 48–55. See also Illinois Initiative on Transparency in Learning and Teaching, https://www.aacu.org/publications-research/periodicals/transparency-teaching-faculty-share-data-and-improve-students.

Grammar Boot Camp—https://docs.google.com/presentation/d/13Qoh1Uzk TYP8jJojMAguv27KC8rO4aTVgn1SXNuT9T4/edit?usp=sharing

Vocab Template—https://docs.google.com/presentation/d/1Vu3M-E9KC-wpyhcREW8KYOX4FQPHjPx3Hc3P3KPfoi4/edit?usp=sharing

Google Classroom Question—https://support.google.com/edu/classroom/answer/6020293?co=GENIE.Platform%3DDesktop&hl=en

LMS Discussion Boards—Canvas—https://community.canvaslms.com/docs/DOC-10727-67952724152

LMS Discussion Boards—Schoology—https://support.schoology.com/hc/en-us/articles/205530658-Course-Materials-Discussions

Parlay—https://parlayideas.com

"Making Online Discussions Meaningful" by Elaine Plybon—https://blog.tcea.org/making-online-discussions-meaningful/

Elaine Plybon's Twitter—https://twitter.com/eplybon

Google Slide Example—https://docs.google.com/presentation/d/1ceUmZmd 4x76bJnv4T6E6SISonuU3yU-3vzDpUN_lye8/edit?usp=sharing

HyperDocs—https://www.hyperdocs.co

HyperDocs Free Templates—https://www.hyperdocs.co/blog/posts/hyper-docs-templates-for-getting-started

Basic HyperDoc Lesson Plan Template—https://docs.google.com/document/d/1l5hNakSEYB8R1uqgX2Gms6xhCjKiaFA7l3xWzMtIFOo/edit

Kate Stevens' Twitter—https://twitter.com/kateteaching?lang=en

Chapter 4
Apply, Create, Explore

The great aim of education is not knowledge but action.

—*Herbert Spencer*

I n a typical lesson, whether synchronous or asynchronous, I'll introduce new content, then ask the students to apply their understanding, create a product or project, or explore and reflect on additional information as a means for assessing their understanding.

There are so many tools that can be used for this portion of the lesson regardless of what content area you teach.

The important thing is not to get overwhelmed; just because there are so many great tools that you could use, it doesn't mean you should use them all. Remember, it's the content knowledge and learning targets that matter, not the EdTech tool.

I recommend choosing one or two tools that you think will best help meet your needs, use that tool until you and your students have mastered it, then consider introducing something else.

With that said, here are some of my favorite EdTech tools and lesson ideas for the "apply, create, explore" portion of a lesson or unit.

MAKE A VIDEO

- **WeVideo**—Video and podcast creation and editing tool that can be used independently or collaboratively. You can record your videos directly within the platform from your laptop or Chromebook.

  This is my preferred video editing tool. It is a little more complex than the next two mentioned in this list but has so much more functionality (think green screen, slow-mo, audio layering). It is great for advanced or extended projects (i.e. school announcements, book trailers, documentaries).

  The free version is watermarked and the premium version includes lots of great stock images, videos, and sounds.

- **Adobe Spark**—Very intuitive video building tool that allows you to search for copyright-free images and icons directly within the program to add to your video. Custom video content must be prerecorded and uploaded, however, so you will have to use it in combination with your computer's camera tool or a screen recording tool like Screencastify.

  There are free and premium versions and special pricing for education.

- **Biteable**—Create quick, easy, animated videos from their stock animation collection. Add music from their collection or upload your own and then add text captions. Great for short explanatory videos.

  The free version includes watermarks.

Lesson Plan

Subject: English

Direct Instruction: Story Arc

Application: Using WeVideo, independently or in groups of up to three people, create a silent film in five scenes. Each scene should depict one stage of the story arc (exposition, rising action, climax, falling action, resolution).

WRITE A BOOK

- **Book Creator**—Digital picture book creator with text, images, shapes, illustration, and audio narration. Teachers invite students to create books within their "classroom library" so the teacher can monitor progress in real time. Books can be shared via a link or downloaded as a PDF.

  The free version gives teachers one library and 40 books.

- **Pixton**—Digital comic book creator. Students can create comic versions of themselves, fictional, or historical characters and create scenes, strips, or entire comic books to be shared via a link or downloaded as an image.

Lesson Plan

Subject: American History
Direct Instruction: Watergate

Application: Use Pixton to create a comic strip portraying Richard Nixon having a conversation with his top advisor the morning the Watergate story broke. You will have to imagine and fictionalize what that conversation sounded like based on the facts we learned about in class. Use three or more scenes. Figure 4.1 shows a sample Pixton comic.

Figure 4.1: Pixton comic.

The free version provides limited options for comic backgrounds, facial expressions, poses, etc. The premium version gives full access to all features.

DESIGN AN INFORMATIONAL GRAPHIC

- **Canva**—Drag and drop professional graphic design tool with templates for infographics, posters, presentations, T-shirts and more. Canva is full of custom templates, images, fonts, and icons.

  Typically some features on Canva are free and others are premium; however, Canva recently announced an education initiative, where licensed teachers can create a Canva Classroom, invite students to join, and then students and teachers have free access to all features.

- **Adobe Spark**—Not just a video tool, Adobe Spark also has simple and intuitive creation tools for posters and websites.

  There are free and premium versions of and special pricing for education.

Lesson Plan
Subject: Math
Direct Instruction: Percentages

Assignment: Using a Canva infographic template, create an infographic called "Items in the Room" (use a room at home for remote learners or the classroom for in-person learners). Find a category of items in the room, count them, then create a percentage for a certain group, that is, 30% of the books in the room are yellow.

Depict at least three category percentages in your infographic.

REVIEW VOCABULARY

- **Quizlet**—Flash card based review website. Teachers can create vocabulary-based flash card decks to share with students, or students can create their own. Quizlet offers programs that help students learn and practice words including quizzes and games.

   Most features can be used free, but premium teachers can track their class's participation and progress.

- **Word Wall**—Takes simple vocabulary or question/answer questions and turns them into arcade-style games, including a knockoff version of Pac-Man. Teachers can create games for students to play by sharing a link, then track their progress in real time.

   The free version gives teachers a limited number of games they can create whereas the premium subscription is unlimited.

Lesson Plan

Subject: Science
Direct Instruction: Climate Change

Lesson: Read the attached article on climate change. Identify 10 good vocab words from the article and use them to create a new set of vocabulary words on Quizlet. Practice and play using those words for at least 20 minutes.

Take a screenshot of your final game score and attach it to this assignment.

PLAY A GAME

- **Deck Toys**—Allows teachers to create self-paced student activities built on a game board. Each activity along the path must be completed before students can "finish the game." Like obstacles in the way of completing a quest.

  The free version allows teachers to create their own games to play with students or reuse other teachers' games that have been made public. The premium version gives access to premium "private" games.

- **Flippity**—Works in combination with a Google Sheet template to create numerous games including matching, scavenger hunts, board games, bingo, word scrambles, crossword puzzles, and many more.

  One of the best features of Flippity is it is entirely free; however, there is no live student data tracking on the back end, so if you don't have all your students in the classroom, you won't be able to guarantee they are working on it in real time. However, I often ask students to screenshot their games and submit those as evidence of their work.

- **Baamboozle**—Is a team-based, Jeopardy-style review game. The teacher can create or reuse games and then facilitate the game for the class. Baamboozle helps in keeping score and displaying the questions.

  The free version allows four teams and 24 questions per game, the premium version allows more.

- **Oodlu**—Is a video game–style review site, where teachers can input vocabulary or question+answers into their program, then choose the style of game for students to play (i.e. space invaders, digital pinball, etc). Whenever students get an answer wrong, they must answer one of your content questions. Be warned, the games are hard! This is probably best suited for older students who have some practice playing online games.

There is a free version with limited access to game styles and a premium version with full access.

Bring it back to the building

GOOSECHASE EDU

This program is an "in real life" scavenger hunt game where students are asked to submit a picture of themselves in different locations, with different objects, or in different contexts. There is also a teacher library where you can reuse games or browse for ideas on how you might use it for your content area.

The free version allows you to run one game at a time with up to five teams, the premium version allows you more teams.

Lesson Plan
Subject: Foreign Language
Topic: Vocabulary

Lesson: Using **GooseChase**, break up the class into five teams. Each item will be a vocabulary word in the foreign language. Students must translate the word/s, then take a photo of themselves with the place or object that word/s described.

CREATE A PRODUCT

- **Thinglink**—Starts with users selecting a preexisting image/video or taking their own, then placing pins onto the image where they would like to add additional content, such as audio narration, an additional image, or a link to a webpage.

  Thinglink is great for teachers to create student-directed exploration lessons, but it's even better if your students are creating their own interactive images, and conducting research to give further information. The free version allows any user to create public content, whereas the premium version allows teachers to create a classroom of students where they can view the work privately.

- Google hack—If you like the idea of Thinglink but don't want to create a premium subscription, you can upload your photos to Google Slides, insert shapes onto the image, then link those shapes to other slides in the presentation or websites. It won't look as professional, but it will essentially perform the same function.

PREBUILT CONTENT REVIEW WEBSITES

- **Khan Academy**—Although Khan was once known as a math review site, they are rapidly expanding into all content areas including grammar, reading, US history, biology, chemistry, and physics, with excellent video-based instruction, auto-graded practice, and assessment. Students can work at their own skill level and pace.

  Khan is always free, but please donate!

- **IXL**—IXL is a massive practice and review platform, with hundreds of activities for every grade level and standard in math, science, language arts, and social studies. Questions are auto-graded, and students are prompted to learn with an example if they are struggling.

  The premium subscription is quite pricey, but anyone can complete 10 questions/day on the site, which is sometimes all you need for a quick review with students.

PRACTICE USING DIGITIZED WORKSHEETS

- **Teacher Made**—Teacher Made makes the digitization of worksheets easy. Simply upload your worksheet as a PDF, then use the toolbar to click onto the section of the worksheet where students typically write their answer, and you can add a digital response. Students can type short answers, select multiple choice, and even leave text and video comments. You can also create self-grading worksheets, so students receive immediate feedback.

  Teacher Made is currently completely free.

- **HyperDocs**—If you don't already have a printed or PDF worksheet you want to use, then I highly recommend moving away from what we understand a worksheet to be and consider creating a HyperDoc instead. HyperDocs aim to transform the learning experience by directing students through a process of engagement, exploration, explanation, application, sharing, reflection, and extension by inserting interactive elements and linking directly into a Google Doc or Slide.

  HyperDocs are completely free to use and reuse. Templates can be found on their website as well as on Facebook and Twitter.

VIRTUAL "ESCAPE ROOMS"

Although virtual escape rooms could probably fall under the "game" section, I think they deserve their own section because they are just that awesome.

Creating custom classroom escape rooms has become a popular trend in education because they are high energy, collaborative, require problem-solving skills, get students moving and talking, and can be created for any subject or content area (see Figure 4.2).

Figure 4.2: Virtual escape room example.

Although often my escape rooms are delivered in person and require hidden clues and invisible ink scattered across the classroom, they can easily be adapted to an online environment.

The foundation of a virtual escape room is using the "response validation" feature of a Google Form. This requires the user (students) to type in an exact number or word before they can submit their answer, or a "code." If they don't have the exact number or word correct, the Google Form will give them an error message and prevent them from moving on.

Once students have the correct code, they can move onto the next section, which is often another puzzle and code. In the end, the final section celebrates their "escape."

How students find their code word and how to integrate that with your content area requires a little bit of creativity. The important piece of these activities is they require students to think critically and problem solve.

Puzzle Ideas:

- Find or create an image with the code word or number on it, and use **Jigsaw Planet** to create an actual, digital puzzle that students have to piece together.

- Give students a key of numbers or letters that correspond to other colors, shapes, or hieroglyphics. Then, provide students with a series of problems that result in the answers giving students the correct colors, shapes, numbers, or letters they will need to solve the code (Figure 4.3).

- Give students a "fill-in-the-blank" question and a link to a YouTube video. The students will need to watch the video and listen closely to hear the phrase with the missing code word.

- Change the size, font, or formatting of single letters in a paragraph or article. Students will have to identify which letters are different, collect them, then unscramble them to create a code word.

- Create a matching game with vocabulary words, where one set has numbers and the other letters. The numbers will indicate which order the letters go in to create the code.

Figure 4.4 shows an example of a virtual escape room I made for my students using a Google Site and Google Form (feel free to play and see if you can escape!).

When doing a virtual escape room activity with my students over Google Meet, I break my students into small groups using the Google Meet breakout room button and then drop the link to the Google Form in the chat box with little to no instruction. The students race to be the first group to "break out" of

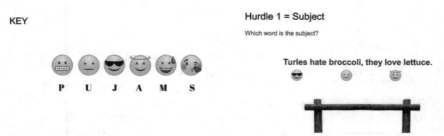

Figure 4.3: Virtual escape room emoji key.

Figure 4.4: Logical Fallacies virtual escape room.

the room. I know students are finished, because on the final section of the form I ask them to return to the main room and type a secret word into the chat box.

Regardless of where the students are, this game is always a favorite and elicits more conversation and participation than any other activity we do, especially from students who I don't typically see take an active leadership role in class.

When the time is up, we always come back together as a whole class and review each puzzle and code together. That way, students can ask questions about the content or I can clarify misconceptions.

For a full tutorial on how to create Google Forms escape rooms, visit the EdTech Toolbox section in Chapter 18, Going Further....

Bring it back to the building

I break my students up into small table groups, post the link to the escape room on Google Classroom, and play ominous or suspenseful music as a timer counts down on the projector. If students "break out" before the clock hits zero, they are directed to raise their hands and whisper a secret word to me, then I usually give each member of that group a piece of candy.

RESOURCES

Items in **bold** in the text are listed here in the Resources. Direct access to all the following resources is available at https://hybridteacherresource.com and on this book's page on www.wiley.com.

WeVideo—https://www.wevideo.com

Adobe Spark—https://spark.adobe.com/sp/

Biteable—https://app.biteable.com

Book Creator—https://bookcreator.com

Pixton—https://www.pixton.com

Canva—https://www.canva.com/education/

Quizlet—https://quizlet.com/latest

Word Wall—https://wordwall.net

Deck Toys—https://deck.toys/dashboard

Flippity—https://www.flippity.net

Baamboozle—https://www.baamboozle.com

Oodlu—https://oodlu.org/home

GooseChase Edu—https://www.goosechase.com/edu/

Thinglink—https://www.thinglink.com

Khan Academy—https://www.khanacademy.org

IXL—https://www.ixl.com

Teacher Made—https://teachermade.com

HyperDocs—https://hyperdocs.co

Jigsaw Planet—https://www.jigsawplanet.com

Chapter 5
Keep Design in Mind

Design is not just what it looks like and feels like. Design is how it works.
—Steve Jobs

As teachers, we adopt many roles, and in the world of digital learning becoming a graphic designer is among them.

In both chapters on synchronous and asynchronous learning, I demonstrate how I use Google Slides or PowerPoint presentations to facilitate lessons. Making those slides look fun and engaging may seem like a frivolous task, but in my experience students are more likely to engage in a lesson that looks exciting and interesting, just like you have a greater appetite for an attractive plate of Christmas dinner than a pile of gruel.

According to Dr. Chaoyan Dong's thesis titled "Positive Emotions and Learning: What Makes the Difference in Multimedia Design?" he states, "when positive emotions are elicited through an aesthetically-pleasing interface design, it can result in deeper learning, at least for low prior knowledge learners."

If you are now thinking, "Gah! I don't have time to make beautiful slides on top of everything else!" don't worry. Described here are tools that make creating visually engaging lessons quick and easy.

SLIDE PRESENTATION RESOURCES

Slide Templates

If you take only one resource away from this section, let it be this. There are plenty of websites where you can download beautiful slide templates for free. I tend to choose one design for a unit, and either create all my lessons in the same slide deck (synchronous lesson) or I'll save the original copy as a "Unit x: TEMPLATE" in my Google Drive, then "file" and "make a copy" of it for each asynchronous lesson.

In this way each unit is "branded" with a specific design, and when we change units there is a clear visual cue for students.

Here are my top three slide template websites:

- **Slides Go** (see Figure 5.1)
- **Slides Carnival**
- **Slides Mania**

Stay Creative

Multi-purpose

Figure 5.1: Slides Go template.

If you are not using a slide template and are instead trying to create a custom slide deck, consider using one of the following websites to download a background image for your slides.

- **Cool Backgrounds** (see Figure 5.2)
- **Transparent Textures**

Once you have a background image downloaded to your computer, you can edit the "master slide" (from the toolbar click "Slide" and "Edit master) on Google Slides and upload your custom image as the background. Then, each of your slides will default to use that background. (See Figure 5.3.)

Fonts

If you are using a slide design template from one of these websites, it will come preloaded with beautiful fonts; but for Google Slide users who are starting

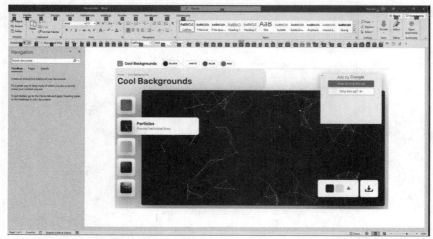

Figure 5.2: Cool Backgrounds.

Figure 5.3: Upload Cool Backgrounds to Google Slides.

from scratch, you'll notice your font options are somewhat limited. You can select the "More Fonts" option at the top of your drop-down menu, or use one of the resources below to really take your fonts to the next level.

- **Text Giraffe** is a website that bills itself as a "logo maker," but it is fantastic for creating titles for presentations and lessons. Copy/paste those back into your Google Slides or Docs.

- **Extensis Fonts** is a Google Slides add-on and opens as a sidebar with a wide range of creative and fun fonts to use in lessons.

- **Magic Rainbow Unicorns**, another add-on for both Google Slides and Docs, will take any text and turn it into a rainbow-colored gradient automatically.
- **Font Meme** contains links to websites with popular culture fonts such as the "Among Us" and Minions fonts.
- **Font Joy** shows you font pairings that work well together, so you know which to use for your titles and which to use for the body of the slide.

Images

Images are powerful teaching tools, and I try to use as many as possible in my lessons and presentations.

When using images, the first thing we need to consider is copyright. Luckily for teachers, there is a law called the "**Classroom Use Exemption**," which allows teachers to use copyrighted material to share with students *in a classroom environment*. Meaning, if you are seeing your students live in person, you are able to grab images for your lessons right off of Google Images without worry of copyright infringement. The law, however, doesn't currently apply to online learning (although we hope that provision will be included in the future with its increased popularity), meaning it might be a good idea to consider some copyright-free image sources.

Copyright-Free Images

One option, and usually my first step because it is so quick and efficient, is to search for images directly within Google Slides. If you click "Insert," "Image," "Search the Web" you'll have a sidebar on the right-hand side of your screen that will allow you to search Google Images directly within Google Slides, as shown in Figure 5.4. The only images you'll see are copyright free and labeled for reuse.

If you're not finding what you are looking for in Google Slides, you might consider searching for images from one of the following websites, all of which offer **Creative Commons** photos and clip art that you can use in your lessons:

- **Unsplash**
- **Pixabay**
- **Pexels**
- **Pics4Learning**

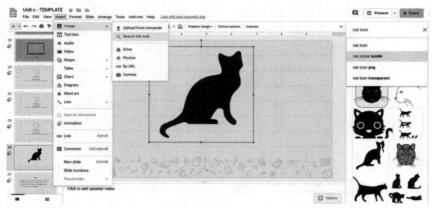

Figure 5.4: Insert images to Google Slides.

Icons

Similar to images, icons can be a great visual learning tool and can help keep your presentations sleek and consistent. Here are several great icon options:

- **Flaticon**—Google Slides extension for free/premium icons and images.
- **The Noun Project**—Website with thousands of easily searchable icons. Free to use if you cite the source, or freely usable with a subscription (discounts for educators).
- **Avataaars**—Cute, cartoon avatars. Download a free file to Dropbox and copy/paste avatars into your slides. Better yet, create a **custom avatar** and copy/paste directly from the website.
- **Open Peeps** and **Humaaans**—Made by the same creator as Avataaars, these icons each have their own unique style; some icons can be downloaded or copied from the website or the entire collection can be downloaded for free or by donation.
- **Blush**—Beautiful, modern hand-drawn icons, images, and scenes that you can customize. Some are free, some are premium.
- **Icon Scout**—Free and premium icons, including popular brand icons.
- **Openclipart**—Free "clip art" style icons.
- **Heritage Library**—Provides free downloads of vintage style images and icons.

Emojis

Although we typically associate emojis with texting or commenting on our phones, emojis can be inserted anywhere there is a text field. Many computers already have an emoji keyboard installed (try right clicking your mouse or track-pad, and look for the word "Emoji Keyboard" in your menu options.) If you don't have an emoji keyboard, you can use the website **Get Emoji** to search for, then copy/paste emojis.

Consider replacing bullet points with smiley faces, using emojis to indicate key elements, and again, you can paste emojis into your "Topics" or instructions in Google Classroom or other learning management systems.

Gifs

Whether you call them gifs or jifs, here are a few ways to make finding these funny moving images even easier, or even create your own:

- **Gif Extension**—Can be added to your Chrome browser, and it will allow you to search for gifs, then click, hold, drag, and drop them directly onto your presentations. By adding the word "transparent" to the end of your search, you can overlay gifs over your entire slide to make it look like the image is moving across the text.

- **GIPHY**—Is a great website for finding gifs but also the site I use to create my own gifs based on videos we've watched as a class. Simply insert a YouTube link into the site, select the portion of the clip you'd like to repeat, upload to GIPHY. When the gif is complete, copy the link to insert into your slides. You can do this with any video, even videos of yourself or students.

- **Google Slides Creator Studio**—Is a Google Slides add-on that allows you to create custom gifs. Many teachers use this tool in combination with their Bitmojis by placing their Bitmoji on the first slide, then duplicating that slide and moving the Bitmoji slightly. Repeating these steps until the Bitmoji has completed an action (i.e. moving across the slide), then opening Creator Studio and clicking the "gif" feature will take each slide and compile them into one moving image to download.

- **Unscreen**—Is great if you want to make live action gifs of yourself. Simply take a short video and upload it to Unscreen. The program will remove the background so you can overlay it on your slides and turn it into a gif file.

Using Your Own Pictures

Sometimes the images we want to share with students can't be found on a website or extension because they are personal pictures we have taken.

We all have different methods for getting pictures to where we want them (emailing them to ourselves, downloading them from Facebook or Instagram, flash drives?!). Here are two super quick ways to get pictures from your phone to your lessons.

Clip Drop

Clip Drop is an AR (augmented reality) copy/paste app.

"What the heck does that mean?" you might be wondering.

When you download the app onto your phone, you can take a picture with your phone camera, then hold your phone up to your computer and that image will be instantly transferred to your desktop.

The free version gives you a certain number of images before it asks you to purchase a monthly/yearly membership.

Google Drive App

If you like the idea of quickly transferring images you take with a phone to your computer, and you use a Google for Education account, I cannot stress enough the importance of the Google Drive App.

Download the app to your phone, then when you want to take a picture for a Google Slide deck lesson, open the Drive app, find the big plus sign "+" in the bottom right corner, then select "use camera" to take a photo or video that will save itself directly to your Drive.

From your Google Slides (Docs or Form) click "Insert," "Image," "From Drive" and you'll be able to add that picture or video directly to the lesson in one click. So easy.

Remove Background

Have some great images you want to share with your students, but there is an embarrassing mess in your kitchen behind you? Or you simply can't find a simple clean backdrop for your photos? Websites like **Remove BG** allow you to upload your images and the programs will automatically cut out the background and replace it with a transparent one, so you can insert an image of yourself right into the middle of a Shakespearean scene or Amazon jungle, or just over your nice custom slide background. (See Figure 5.5.)

Figure 5.5: Original image and image on Remove BG.

Other Design Tools

- **Canva for Education**—Canva created the first of its kind in professional-grade design templates. I love to use Canva for creating bookmarks, posters, and invitations for school events, but I mainly use it as a teaching tool, where students are using Canva to create posters, info-graphics and presentations. (See more on Canva in Chapter 4, Apply, Create, Explore.)

- **Projector**—Presentation, poster, and social media templates with fun design elements. Currently completely free.

- **Genially**—Presentation templates with fun animation and even interactive elements. Free with the option for a premium upgrade.

Colors

My most used color tool is a Chrome extension called **Eye Dropper**, shown in Figures 5.6 and 5.7. When I have a colorful image and I'd like to use that same color for my font or background, I use the Eye Dropper extension to identify the HEX code of that color, and then copy/paste into the "custom" color field.

Use the Eye Dropper and click the shirt to select the coral shirt color. Then copy the HEX code.

Figure 5.6: Selecting a color with Eye Dropper.

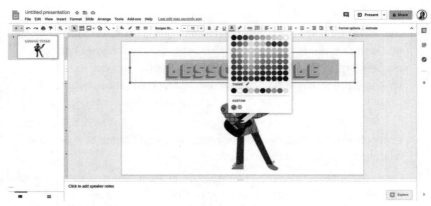

Figure 5.7: Adding a custom color with Eye Dropper.

Select your text, click the color icon, and then the "+" at the bottom under "custom" to paste the HEX code in and use your matching color.

To help you pick visually appealing color combinations for your slide decks, websites, or HyperDocs, a website like **Coolors** can help you to create a complementary color palette.

However, we also need to consider access and make sure that our color combinations are accessible for students with color blindness, visual impairments, or dyslexia. Web AIM (Web Accessibility in Mind) and **Accessible Color Generator** both have color-checking features that allow you to input your chosen colors, and the program will give you an accessibility score or recommendations for more appropriate combinations.

CONSIDER COGNITIVE LOAD

We want to make our lessons look fun and engaging for our students, and using premade slide templates, professional images, icons, and backgrounds gives us a big boost when it comes to creating visually appealing lessons, but there is a danger in having "too much of a good thing" when it comes to engaging lesson designs, as we need to consider our students' capacity for taking in new information (whether that be images, videos, text, or graphics).

Cognitive load theory was developed by John Sweller in 1988, who concluded that there is only so much information that a person can process in their "working memory" at any given time.

A study on cognitive load in multimedia learning, by Richard E. Mayer and Roxanna Moreno, claims that cognitive load should be a central consideration when designing multimedia learning materials.

Mayer and Moreno give several suggestions on how to reduce cognitive load:

- **Use Narration**—When there are too many instructions to present simply via text, consider recording them either by video or audio. **Screencastify** will allow you to screen record yourself delivering instructions via video, and **Pear Deck** has a great audio recording feature so that students can listen to instructions or narration when working through their lessons independently.

- **Segmenting**—More slides with less information on each is always better than fewer slides with more information. I cannot stress this enough. Chunk your lessons so that each slide follows the common design principle "rule of three." Have no more than three bullet points or three major visual elements on any one slide.

- **Pretraining**—Mayer and Moreno acknowledge that occasionally there will be a portion of a lesson that is difficult to segment or narrate (a complicated graph or diagram, for example), and they recommend pretraining (or preteaching) key elements on the prior slides to prepare students for the complexity that follows.

- **Weeding**—Mayer and Moreno suggest "eliminating extraneous material." Keep in mind the idea of "negative space" or the blank spaces on your slides. You want a good amount of it so your slides never look too busy or overwhelming.

- **Signaling**—Consider visual and auditory strategies for signaling the most important pieces of information to students, including emphasis in your speech when narrating and using color, font, and symbols to emphasize key pieces of written instruction or information.

- **Aligning Text and Image**—When using an image that directly corresponds to your text, rather than having students search or scan for the corresponding elements. Place the text directly onto the image or use arrows to indicate the corresponding locations.

- **Eliminating Redundancy**—If you are using narration to deliver content or instructions, you don't need to write it in text. This is especially important for delivering lessons synchronously. Don't put the words you are planning to say on your slides. As mentioned previously, you might decide to include a follow-up slide that signals or reemphasizes key points in text or image, but having two versions (text and audio) of the same information creates competition for cognitive load.

Ultimately there is a balance that teachers need to try to strike between the benefits of making students want to engage in our visually appealing lessons and not overloading them with unnecessary information, as to not take away from the learning.

RESOURCES

Items in **bold** in the text are listed here in the Resources. Direct access to all the following resources is available at https://hybridteacherresource.com and on this book's page on www.wiley.com.

SlidesGo—https://slidesgo.com

Slides Carnival—https://www.slidescarnival.com

Slides Mania—https://slidesmania.com

Cool Backgrounds—https://coolbackgrounds.io

Transparent Textures—https://www.transparenttextures.com

Text Giraffe—https://www.textgiraffe.com

Extensis Fonts—https://gsuite.google.com/marketplace/app/extensis_fonts/568288816452

Magic Rainbow Unicorns—https://gsuite.google.com/marketplace/app/magic_rainbow_unicorns_slides/727496290931

Font Meme—https://fontmeme.com

Font Joy—https://fontjoy.com

Classroom Use Exemption—https://www.lib.umn.edu/copyright/limitations#classroomuse

Creative Commons—https://creativecommons.org

Unsplash—https://unsplash.com

Pixabay—https://pixabay.com

Pexels—https://www.pexels.com

Pics4Learning—https://www.pics4learning.com

Flaticon—https://www.flaticon.com

The Noun Project—https://thenounproject.com

Avataaars—https://avataaars.com

Custom Avataaar—https://getavataaars.com/?topType=LongHairFroBand

Open Peeps—https://www.openpeeps.com

Humaaans—https://www.humaaans.com

Blush—https://blush.design

Icon Scout—https://iconscout.com/popular-icons

Openclipart—https://openclipart.org

Heritage Library—https://www.heritagetype.com/collections/free-vintage-illustrations

Get Emoji—https://getemoji.com

Gif extension—https://chrome.google.com/webstore/detail/gif-extension/pnpapokldhgeofbkljienpjofgjkafkm/related

GIPHY—https://giphy.com

Google Slides Creator Studio—https://gsuite.google.com/marketplace/app/creator_studio/509621243108

Unscreen—https://www.unscreen.com

Remove BG—https://www.remove.bg

Canva for Education—https://www.canva.com/education/

Projector—https://projector.com/home/

Genially—https://www.genial.ly

Eye Dropper—https://chrome.google.com/webstore/detail/eye-dropper/hmdcmlfkchdmnmnmheododdhjedfccka?hl=en

Coolors—https://coolors.co

Web AIM—https://webaim.org/resources/contrastchecker/

Accessible Color Generator—https://learnui.design/tools/accessible-color-generator.html

Cognitive Load Theory—https://www.sciencedirect.com/science/article/pii/B9780123876911000028

Cognitive Load Theory Study—http://www.theurbanclimatologist.com/uploads/4/4/2/5/44250401/mayermoreno2003reducingcognitive-overload.pdf

Screencastify—https://www.screencastify.com

Pear Deck—https://www.peardeck.com

Chapter 6
Project-Based Learning

You can teach a person all you know, but only experience will convince him that what you say is true.

—Richelle E. Goodrich

Project-based learning assignments (PBL) ask students to engage with real-world problems as they use standard aligned skills to design and implement solutions.

I first used project-based learning in 2016 while I was teaching in a brick-and-mortar school in Las Vegas through an assignment called "180 Days to Change the World." Student groups were asked to identify a problem in our community, research it, and implement a project to help solve that problem.

Every few weeks we would dedicate a day in class to creating benchmarks, checking in, and meeting in groups to work on our projects. The project spanned the course of the year and we incorporated the skills we were learning in class, such as conducting research, letter writing, and persuasion, into our PBL.

The results were inspiring: students held fundraisers, developed a school recycling program, baked dog biscuits, and cleaned up their parks. (See Figure 6.1.)

Students fundraised to provide snack bags for the local homeless community

Students wrote and delivered encouraging messages to a local children's hospital.

Figure 6.1: Photo documentation of project-based learning.

Although PBL is fantastic in a traditional school setting, possibilities for learning expand when students are remote. Whereas building a compost pile or painting a mural might be difficult to work on while in the classroom, if a student is learning remotely a few days a week there is more time and potential for engaging in PBL in their communities.

You might consider dedicating one day each week or every few weeks to allow students to work on their PBL. Schedule check-ins with individual students or groups to help hold them accountable for staying on top of their milestones.

One of the best parts of PBL is its capacity to be cross-curricular. Students are often using the scientific method to design a project or process, measure data and results, as well as research, communicate, and reflect. Science, math, and English are rolled into one.

Here are a few examples of popular PBL assignments:

- Redesign coastal cities for sea level rise.
- Study local land regions and resources to identify a geological-based response to the Zombie Apocalypse.
- Redesign a school space.

Although the concept of PBL is appealing to many educators, it is often hard to know where to begin or find the time to fit it into the curriculum.

START WITH SPRINTS

PBL is deeply ingrained in the design thinking process. John Spencer, educator and author of *Launch,* defines **design thinking** as, "The premise of tapping into student curiosity and allowing them to create, test and re-create until they eventually ship what they made to a real audience."

That process of creating, testing, and re-creating is essential in project-based learning, but you don't need to launch into an entire unit devoted to PBL to give it a try. Instead, you start with something called a "design sprint": a short challenge that can be completed in a class period, where students are introduced to a problem, then guided through a process that helps them create a viable solution.

I was first introduced to design sprints by Les McBeth from Future Design School at the Google Certified Innovator Academy in an activity that I have since adapted to use with my students.

Design Sprint

Challenge:
Rethink the sitting experience. This could be any place or circumstance in which we sit: at school, on an airplane, on the couch.

Process:

1. *Identify a problem* students have with sitting or seats.
2. *Develop multiple ideas* that could solve that problem.
3. Choose one idea and *sketch three iterations* or versions of that solution.
4. Choose the best version and *prototype* it using paper or aluminum foil.
5. Partner with another student or group and *give and receive feedback* to each other by asking questions.
6. *Revise* the product based on the feedback received.
7. *Pitch it* to the class by posing the problem and presenting the solution.

Result:
Lots of fun, collaboration, and critical thinking.

Design sprints are a great way to wade into the waters of PBL for both teachers and students. You might consider starting with challenges like redesigning the sitting experience, or one of John Spencer's many video-based

"**Maker Challenge**" prompts such as "Design the Ultimate Roller Coaster" or "Design the Ultimate Tiny House" to practice the design thinking process, then consider how design sprints might apply to your content area.

Lesson Plan
Subject: Science
   Design Sprint: Have your students consider problems associated with climate change and propose solutions.

Subject: History
Design Sprint: Propose a moment in history (or ask students to research and choose their own) when a great invention (i.e. the light bulb) solved a problem (house fires), and ask students to design alternative solutions.

The great thing about design sprints is the sky's the limit. As these solutions or products aren't meant to be created outside of a paper prototype, you can encourage your students to adopt "moon-shot" thinking and invent as creatively as possible without sticking to the realm of what we know is possible.

The other great thing about design thinking is it is as easy to facilitate in a brick-and-mortar classroom as it is over video conferencing (as long as remote students have access to a piece of paper).

RESOURCES

Items in **bold** in the text are listed here in the Resources. Direct access to all the following resources is available at https://hybridteacherresource.com and on this book's page on www.wiley.com.

Design Thinking—https://spencerauthor.com/what-is-design-thinking/

Maker Challenge—https://www.youtube.com/watch?v=zAY5c21EEBU&list=PLzDOGMsmDvetek2wQR1xyCD0SG6ekGU4c

Chapter 7
Executive Functioning Skills

I have always believed that process is more important than results.
—M. S. Dhoni

The past few chapters have explored designing asynchronous, or student-driven learning experiences, which allow students an increased level of agency and flexibility in their learning. However, posting an asynchronous assignment and expecting complete engagement from a class of K-12 students isn't realistic, as our students are still in the process of developing their executive functioning skills.

According to the **Center on the Developing Child** at Harvard University, "Executive function and self-regulation skills are the mental processes that enable us to plan, focus attention, remember instructions, and juggle multiple tasks successfully." Helping students develop their executive functioning skills is important for all ages and learning environments, but it becomes particularly critical when using asynchronous learning, either in the classroom or in a hybrid model.

I am lucky to work with learning interventionist Stacy Denham at PSD Global Academy (PGA), who is an expert in executive functioning skill development and works closely with our students who are struggling with their executive functioning skills. She emphasizes the importance of understanding that students who typically "struggle with school" are often struggling less with the academic component and more with their executive functioning or self-regulation and that these skills need to be explicitly taught and supported by an adult.

At PGA, one of our main jobs is to support parents on how they can support successful executive functioning at home, because building basic foundational practices, such as getting enough sleep, eating nutritional foods, building healthy habits and routines, is an important place to start. (See more on this in Chapter 15, Parent/Guardian Communication.)

However, there is still a lot we can do in the brick-and-mortar and virtual classroom as well.

TIPS FOR TEACHING EXECUTIVE FUNCTIONING SKILLS

Planning

Teach students how to make a plan for their day, week, or period and how to use the tools that can help keep them organized.

Although it might seem obvious to some, many students benefit from a lesson on how to prioritize which work to do first, especially those who have a lot of missing work. Although all the work we assign in school serves a purpose, students who understand how to prioritize higher-value assignments tend to do better. Rather than letting a student who is already far behind and failing spend most of their time turning in low-point-value work, teach students how to identify the assignments that will help their grade most.

Have students make a flowchart using shapes and arrows on a Google Drawing, Google Slide, or PowerPoint slide, for this would be a great mini-lesson to support this executive functioning skill (see Figure 7.1).

Once students have identified the work they are planning to complete, the best practice is to write down their plan. Many schools provide paper planners to students, and teachers can model how to put assignments into our planners and provide time during our lessons for students to do so.

Although using a paper planner is a great skill and works well for many people, I also like to give my students digital organization options as well and show students how to add events to their Google Calendars or how to make a "To Do" list using a note-taking app, such as **Keep**.

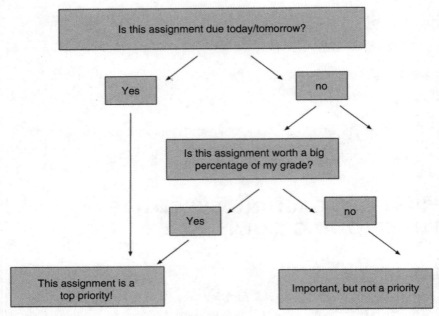

Figure 7.1: Work prioritization flowchart.

Time Management

Students almost never manage their own time while at a brick-and-mortar school. Teachers tell them when to start and when to stop; bells tell them when to move from class to class and when to go home; yet time management is an important skill to develop.

Using timers is a great way for students to manage how long they spend on any given task. When I am planning an asynchronous lesson, I like to give students an estimated amount of time I think a task will take to complete, then provide a link to a timer so that the student can start it at the beginning of the lesson. Students know that if they finish far before the timer goes off, they probably need to go back and dig a little deeper into the lesson or add more. But, if the timer goes off way before they are done, they should email me and I can either help them finish or give them a shortened version of the assignment.

If you don't embed a timer in your lessons, you might want to encourage your students to use a timer that works best for them. Timer choices include their phone, a smart speaker (e.g. Alexa), or by simply Googling "10-minute timer," a new timer will start.

Task Initiation

When no one is forcing you to get started on a piece of work, it is tough for *anyone* to initiate the task! Let alone a K-12 student.

School psychologist Peg Dawson suggests that for students who struggle with task initiation, starting with small, easy tasks is a good place to start (that's why so many of us choose to start our day reading email!).

I like to post "Do Now" or "Bell Ringer" assignments for students that are quick, easy, and fun. If that feels like an approachable first task, the student is more likely to complete the next, longer assignment.

For students who are really struggling with task initiation, Dawson also recommends asking them to create a list of their barriers or obstacles and then brainstorm possible solutions or strategies to help overcome them.

Organization

Sometimes not doing the work is a simple matter of not being able to find the work to do. I've already mentioned the importance of teachers keeping an organized and consistent manner of posting work in their learning management system, but it is also important that students are responsible for certain pieces of work, and they keep them well organized.

In a brick-and-mortar classroom, it might mean discussing and brainstorming best practices for keeping their backpacks, desks, or lockers organized.

In a virtual learning environment, I always start the year by teaching my students how to bookmark important websites and documents to their browsers, how to organize their files in Google Drive, and how to insert "horizontal lines" or dividers into their Google Docs.

Self-Monitoring

Self-monitoring is the ability to check in with yourself on how you are doing or feeling. Establishing a daily practice of checking in with students and asking them to evaluate how they are doing or feeling isn't just a great way to build community in your classroom, it's also a good way to teach students how to regularly self-monitor.

Once students can identify their emotions, we also need to make sure they have the strategies in place to address them including taking a deep breath, taking a break, or asking for help (either in person by raising a hand or online by emailing or messaging the teacher).

See more on self-monitoring in Chapter 8, Social and Emotional Learning.

Attentional Control

As a young student myself, I remember teachers telling the class to "pay attention," but I now understand that keeping our minds on task is not an innate skill, and I was never explicitly taught how.

Introducing mindfulness, or "mindful moments," into your lessons is one way to teach and train your students' brains to focus. Mindfulness is a scientifically supported, secular practice that helps to teach students how to notice when their attention has drifted away and bring it back to what they should be focusing on. For more on mindfulness, see Chapter 8, Social and Emotional Learning.

There are also apps and extensions designed to help you stay focused and on task including:

- **Stay Focused**—allows you to set time limits for websites you spend too much time on (i.e. new sites or social media).

- **Forest**—takes the concept of blocking distracting sites and gamifies it by allowing users to "plant" a digital tree once they begin working, which will grow as long as the user stays on task, but dies if the user visits a distracting site. Users can grow forests of digital trees through the app or extension.

- **Just Read**—when turned on, this extension eliminates the ads from a website, allowing the user a distraction-free, focused online reading experience.

Now, take a good look at that list (paying attention, starting tasks, staying organized), and ask yourself if you are still working on any of these skills as a fully grown adult?

I know I sure am.

So we need to bring that empathy to our students, with their much less developed prefrontal cortexes, and remember that when a student doesn't start their work or pay attention, it's not necessarily because they don't care, but it is a skill that still needs to be developed—and it is our job to teach these skills.

In Chapter 16, Technology Bootcamp, I discuss a one-week course that we use at PGA to start the year, focused on teaching students about the tools they will need to know how to use to be successful in class as they get to know each other and their teachers. We also focus on introducing some strategies to help develop executive functioning skills. As the course is asynchronous, it also gives us the opportunity to identify the students whose executive functioning skills are lagging and start interventions early to try to provide those students the support they'll need to be successful in our model.

RESOURCES

Items in **bold** in the text are listed here in the Resources. Direct access to all the following resources is available at https://hybridteacherresource.com and on this book's page on www.wiley.com.

Center on the Developing Child—https://developingchild.harvard.edu/science/key-concepts/

Keep—https://keep.google.com/

Stay Focused—https://chrome.google.com/webstore/detail/stayfocusd/laankejkbhbdhmipfmgcngdelahlfoji/related?hl=en

Forest—https://www.forestapp.cc

Just Read—https://chrome.google.com/webstore/detail/just-read/dgmanlpmmkibanfdgjocnabmcaclkmod?hl=en

Chapter 8
Social and Emotional Learning

Some of the greatest moments in human history were fueled by emotional intelligence.

—Adam Grant

In Chapter 7 I explored executive function skills, which go hand in hand with the strategies in social and emotional learning, especially in self-monitoring and paying attention.

If you are a teacher, you know the concept of Bloom's Taxonomy in which students need to have their basic needs met (i.e. nourishment, safety, sense of belonging) before they are able to learn.

In addition, we know through recent advancements in neurobiology that students need to be in the right frame of mind before they can access their "learning brain."

According to Bruce Perry at the Child Trauma Academy, when our brains go through fear responses our IQ drops, and in some cases, we can't get back to our "thinking and understanding brain" for up to two hours.

It is therefore important to make sure students are in a relaxed, parasympathetic state (rest and digest) before we ask them to start learning.

For some students with social anxiety, learning online from home will already put them in a more relaxed state, as they are more comfortable and in control of their environments. In fact, students with severe social anxiety are the fastest growing population we see joining us at PSD Global Academy (PGA), and we've seen tremendous improvements in both their academic and social lives.

However, all students can benefit from learning some skills to help them relax and focus before any lesson, activity, or task.

MINDFULNESS

As you may recall from Chapter 2, Synchronous Learning, in my classroom (both brick-and-mortar and virtual) we start every class with a few deep breaths or a "mindful moment." According to a study by **John Meiklejohn et al.** titled

"Integrating Mindfulness into the K-12 Curriculum," taking deep breaths helps move you into a parasympathetic state, where students are more likely to learn and remember. The practice of mindfulness has also shown to foster resilience in both teachers and students alike. Plus, it is a good strategy for teaching students how to focus (on their breathing) and sets a calm, concentrated tone for class.

However, with my middle school students I need their buy-in before they are able to sincerely practice deep breathing in class with their peers. Many of the strategies I share here I picked up from Meena Srinivasan in her book *Teach, Breathe, Learn*.

Here is how I introduce mindful moments with my classes:

1. We start by defining the problem. I show a video called "**Release**" by Julie Bayer Salzman, where middle schoolers are discussing the stressors they feel in their everyday lives. The testimonials are accompanied by intense music and flashing images, creating an overall feeling of mounting stress and anxiety. I pause the video at 2:21, at the height of the tension, and ask students if anyone can relate to any of these feelings. Most students will raise their hands, and some will elaborate on what stressors they have in their lives. Sometimes I have students do a quick write/reflection here about what causes them stress or anxiety. Then I finish the video, which moves into a calm mindfulness exercise. I don't ask students to follow along, but I do, and many will as well. When the video is finished, I ask students if they could feel the shift in tone, and if they felt better by the time the video ended. They all agree they do. Then I emphasize how practicing something called "mindfulness" can help us shift into a calm relaxed state when we are feeling the stresses and anxieties in our lives.

2. Next I show the students a video by ASAP Science called "**The Scientific Power of Meditation**" and ask students to write down at least one scientific benefit to meditation that they hear discussed in the video. Then students share in partners and with the whole class.

3. Finally, I gain social buy-in by showing a couple of short clips of celebrities, including Kobe Bryant and Lady Gaga, discussing why they practice mindfulness and how it helps them. Then I ask them to discuss who they recognized in the video and how mindfulness helped them in their singing or basketball careers. We then apply it to our own lives by brainstorming what we do on a daily basis (school, sports, hobbies, family interactions) and how mindfulness might help us.

I spread out these three steps in the buy-in process over three days, three weeks. I've done them live, synchronously and asynchronously. However you choose to deliver the content, if you are planning to implement mindfulness into your routine, it helps to have the students invested.

Once students have bought in, we start doing our "mindful moment" at the start of each synchronous class. Typically I will find a "**breathing gif**" to add to the beginning of my lesson slides, and we will follow along with it. But sometimes we will do a slightly longer mindfulness exercise via a **YouTube video** or on **Headspace** (which provides free premium accounts for teachers).

The beauty of having the student buy in and normalize a deep breath/"mindful moment" is that you can use it to refocus the energy of class whenever you need to. If my students are getting a little too agitated or out of control, I'll ring a little bell I have in the classroom and tell the class that we are going to take a quick "mindful moment" to refocus. This is a great strategy too for an individual student who is experiencing frustration or stress during class.

Mindfulness is an important aspect of my social & emotional teaching strategy, but building relationships and checking in with students are equally important. Read more about social and emotional learning in Chapter 9, Building Culture and Community.

RESOURCES

Items in **bold** in the text are listed here in the Resources. Direct access to all the following resources is available at https://hybridteacherresource.com and on this book's page on www.wiley.com.

Meiklejohn, J., Phillips, C., Freedman, M. et al. (2013). Integrating mindfulness training into K-12 education: Fostering the resilience of teachers and students. *Mindfulness* 3: 291–307. https://doi.org/10.1007/s12671-012-0094-5

Teach, Breathe, Learn by Meena Srinivasan—https://www.meenasrinivasan.com/teach-breathe-learn

"Release" by Julie Bayer Salzman—https://www.youtube.com/watch?v=GVWRvVH5gBQ&feature=emb_logo

"The Scientific Power of Meditation"—https://www.youtube.com/watch?v=Aw71zanwMnY&t=10s

Mindfulness Video Playlist—https://www.youtube.com/playlist?list=PLa6zQc0FTawGheJRtG-JPHdFJr-XH1a_R

Headspace—https://www.headspace.com/educators

Chapter 9
Building Culture and Community

I cannot be a teacher without exposing who I am.

—*Paulo Freire*

Right alongside procedures, norms, and expectations, teachers typically dedicate a portion of their time at the beginning of the year to having the class get to know each other and building a strong classroom community.

According to **Dwyer et al.**, "Fostering a positive climate and sense of community for students in educational settings has been linked with retention and academic success."

In my experience, students learn better from teachers they trust and respect, as well as in environments where they feel safe and comfortable to share ideas and make mistakes.

Brick-and-mortar schoolteachers likely already have a number of activities they use to start the year: name games and brain breaks for when the energy starts to get stale.

What follows are activities for building culture and community using various EdTech tools that can be conducted in person or online.

STARTING THE YEAR

Having a few community building activities to complete in the first week or two are particularly helpful when you are simultaneously putting your students through a tech bootcamp. (See more on this in Chapter 16, Technology Bootcamp.) These activities will help lighten the academic load while your students learn the essential technical skills they will need for the year. They will also provide the opportunity to reinforce some of those tech skills if you incorporate them into your community building activities.

For example, you might plan to use some **Applied Digital Skills** lessons in your technology bootcamp (Applied Digital Skills is a platform with prebuilt, video-based asynchronous lessons designed to teach students practical and digital skills). If so, have your students get to know each other through one of their introductory lessons like Design a Poster About You. Then ask your students to share their posters on Google Classroom or Padlet. This activity will incorporate several tech skills and platforms into a low-stakes, fun, community building activity.

Here are a few more online/remote community building activities I like to use.

Lesson Plans

WRITE A LETTER TO THE TEACHER

After reading about how **Liz Galarza uses dialogue journals** to build student relationships, I now start every year with this activity. I find that most students really appreciate the opportunity to write a personal letter to their teacher all about themselves and are excited that I write a letter back in response.

Typically, I have my students write these on paper and hand them in. If students are coming to campus a few days each week, you could collect them then. If you are in a remote environment, consider giving your students the option to either mail or email their letters.

The benefit of using email is the opportunity to teach that as a skill and get students in the habit of emailing the teacher so it feels more normal or comfortable to do once they have a question they need to ask.

I typically provide students with a **slide deck**, shown in Figure 9.1, to teach proper letter formatting and provide writing prompts for students who are hesitant to get started.

FIRST LETTER!

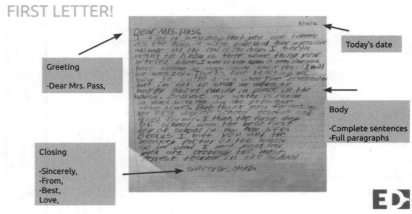

Figure 9.1: Write a letter lesson.

In this activity, you not only get to know your students, but you can also teach them a technical skill, and you have a writing sample from day one that you can refer back to.

CREATE A SCRAPBOOK PAGE

Create a Scrapbook Page is another Applied Digital Skills lesson in which students will be simultaneously learning technical skills (in this case, formatting a Google Slide deck with text and images) and also sharing their interests/learning styles.

One nice feature of Google Slide decks is they can easily be copied/pasted together, so after your students complete their scrapbooks, you could take a page from each student and make a big class scrapbook of interests/hobbies/family/culture/etc. to present to the class, print, or share in a digital space.

You might also ask your students to share a link to their scrapbook page (or an image of it) with the rest of the class so that classmates can start to get to know each other and make connections. Students could post these to the learning management system (LMS) home page, discussion board, or a Padlet.

CREATE A LEARNER PROFILE AND PORTFOLIO

Another great way to start the year is to learn how to create a basic website to use as a learning portfolio. Students are, again, learning valuable technology skills, but they can also use their portfolio to display pieces of work they are proud of as the year progresses.

I often use Google Sites because it is free and the simplest platform I've used to **build a website**. There is, of course, an Applied Digital Skills lesson that can teach your students how to do this or plenty of **YouTube tutorials**.

The first assignment I give to students when setting up their website is to create an "About Me" or "Learner Profile" page, where they can share information about themselves, their families, and their learning styles. (See Figure 9.2.)

Figure 9.2: Learner profile template.

I've adapted a **template Google Site** (Figure 9.3) that you can use with your students for portfolios/learner profiles. Just be sure to make a copy before you use it!

On this template I ask students to:

- Add a banner image that represents them/their interests

  Students can upload an image, find one online, or even create their own using a **Google Drawing template**.

- Type their name, nickname, and pronouns (optional)

  Identifying pronouns is becoming more and more commonplace, and giving students a public place to do so early in the year can help save the embarrassment of the "Are you a boy or a girl?" question. I do not require this, however, as some students might not be ready to identify their gender to the class.

- Link to a short voice recording of how they pronounce their name on Vocaroo.

  Vocaroo is the simplest voice recording tool I've found, and I have been using it for years to capture short student responses. Simply click the big record button on the website, speak, and once you've stopped the recording, Vocaroo (Figure 9.4) provides you with a shareable link.

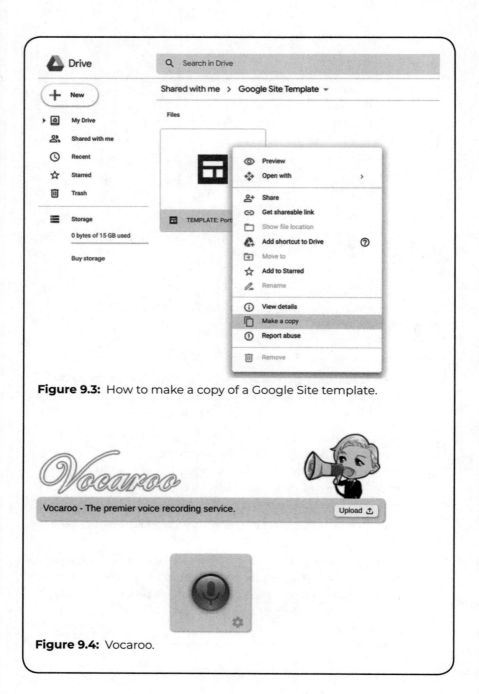

Figure 9.3: How to make a copy of a Google Site template.

Figure 9.4: Vocaroo.

Hearing students pronounce their own names is incredibly beneficial for me, as I believe it is important for the students' sense of belonging and identity to have their names known. Having them in a voice recorded format allows me to refer to the early days of the year if I've forgotten a pronunciation.

- List hobbies and interests

Students add video games, YouTube creators, books, movies, sports, and favorite foods. I encourage them to add interests and hobbies that might allow them to make connections with other classmates.

- Post the results of a learner profile survey, called "True Colors"

High school English teacher, Google Certified Innovator, and Google Educator Group leader **Stephanie Rothstein** introduced me to this assessment of student personality and learning styles in her webinar "**Can We Talk: Personality, Teams, Conversation, and Feedback**." She shares how understanding student learning styles can help you determine how best to group students together and provide feedback that feels motivating and meaningful to them.

The assessment takes only about five minutes to complete on a Google Form, then the answers are directly exported to a Google Sheet that I give students access to, to review their results, and take a screenshot of to add to their learner profile (Figure 9.5).

Students complete their learner profiles asynchronously and then the next time we meet for synchronous class I ask every student to share the links to their sites (either in the chat box or in a Google Classroom Question/discussion board) and we spend some time exploring each other's pages and leaving comments and connections.

Then, we regroup and I talk about the True Colors assessment, briefly outlining what each color represents and emphasizing that each personality type contributes a unique skill set, and that each is necessary for a functioning society.

At this point, I may also put students into breakout rooms (or groups) based on their dominant color and provide discussion questions about whether they agree or disagree with their color assessment or group them based on interests or hobbies they discussed in their learner profiles. Ultimately, one of the biggest benefits of this activity is to create connections between students. Particularly when they are online and

Figure 9.5: True Colors results.

it is harder to make natural, quick connections with each other ("hey, I like your shirt"; "I play that game too"), grouping students based on something they already have in common is a great way to get students to start to feel comfortable with their peers.

The other major benefit to these sites is as a reference of students' interests in case I need to connect with or motivate a particular student in the future. Bookmarking each student's "Learner Portfolio" page in a folder in your browser is an easy way to quickly access them in the future.

Then, continue to update these sites throughout the year by asking students to post finished projects for their portfolios.

PLAY "WOULD YOU RATHER"

One of my favorite in-person games to play is "would you rather," where students move to different sides of the room depending on their answer. To adapt this for a virtual class you could use **Google Jamboard** or another virtual whiteboard, which has draggable features, so students can move their icon or sticky note to the side of the screen they agree with most.

Google Jamboard is a virtual whiteboard that allows you to handwrite (with a touch screen), add notes, and annotate. Because it is a Google file type, it can be used collaboratively and multiple people can contribute at the same time. For this activity I use the "sticky note" feature and create one for each student. They are instructed to move their sticky note to the side of the Jamboard that they agree with and then type their reason into the sticky note for everyone to see (Figure 9.6).

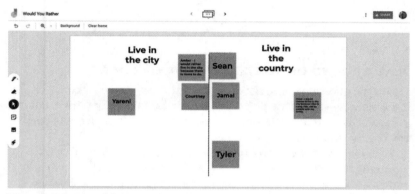

Figure 9.6: Would you rather Jamboard.

I have recently seen an elevated, song-based version of this called "Bop or Flop" where the teacher plays a snippet of a song, and then students drag their sticky note to the "Bop" side of the whiteboard, indicating they like the song, or the "Flop" slide on the whiteboard, indicating they don't. Teachers could preselect the music or ask students to contribute songs they think are "bops" and "flops."

CREATE A GUESSING GAME

At this point, if you've completed a few of these activities, students are starting to get to know quite a bit about each other and possibly making connections. So, just like I would when teaching content, I like to give students a little formative assessment to see how much we know about one another.

One more from Applied Digital Skills, this "**create a guessing game**" lesson teaches students how to make their own quizzes in Google Forms and asks them to make a quiz about themselves for their teacher or classmates to take. For a big class, you could assign students groups to share and take their quizzes in.

This lesson would be a great way to set up your students with the skills for creating their own content-based quizzes later in the year.

PLAY A ROUND OF QUIZIZZ, KAHOOT, OR GIMKIT

Taking the guessing game option to the next level, you could consider using a review-style game platform like **Quizizz**, **Kahoot**, or **Gimkit**, but instead of asking content-based questions, make a question about each one of your students.

Each platform allows you to create new or reuse preexisting questions, typically in a multiple-choice format, where students can play and race against each other for the most points and quickest answers.

When I do this with my class, I first make sure everyone has had ample time to learn about one another (from posters, introductory videos, or learner profiles) then I ask each student to write a quiz question from the information they've already shared with the class. Students enter the question into a **classmate trivia Google Form**. I export their answers to a Google Sheet and then copy/paste their questions and answers into the quiz platform. I thought it would take me a really long time to compile the questions into a quiz game for each class, but it takes me only about 20 minutes, and the effort pays off as students love being the subject matter of a quiz, and it's a great way to build community as a class.

I usually play this game at least two or three times so that we can achieve full mastery, and everyone in the class knows something about someone else.

HAVE A DISCUSSION

Once your students are starting to get comfortable with each other, you might want to introduce different methods for online discussion and practice those tools as you get to know one another better. (Also see the section "Asynchronous Discussion" in Chapter 3.)

Padlet is one of the most versatile discussion platforms that allows students to post and respond to each other in a "bulletin board" format. It is particularly good for short, text-based discussions and sharing photos and links. I love Padlet for super quick community building questions, like "Add a gif to Padlet that represents what you did this summer," or "Add a music video link that describes how you feel about being back in school."

Flipgrid is another great tool for online discussions where students post short videos and video responses to each other on a given topic. As it is entirely video based it feels a little more like having a live discussion where students can see and hear each other, but there is the added benefit of having more time to think and construct a response.

Flipgrid has also offered a **list of community building questions** and activities that you might use to start the year. I like to use Flipgrid for "two truths and a lie" videos.

THE "NORM FORM"

After we've had some time to get to know one another, and a few weeks of class to get into habits and routines, I always take some time for "norming," or setting the expectations for each other about the standard/typical practice in the classroom.

When students are in the brick-and-mortar classroom with me, we often start by playing a dice game. Students are placed in groups and are given a number of dice, then told they need to invent a new game using the dice. After a few minutes, each group has the opportunity to share with the class the game they created. Inevitably students will have made a set of rules for their game, and this leads us into a discussion on why it is important to establish rules or expectations for one another in order to have a fun class experience (i.e. rules enhance fun, not limit it).

If conducting this activity virtually, I put my student groups into breakout rooms and give them a link to **virtual dice** to create their games. They might also be given or asked to create a shared Google Doc to create their list of rules.

From there we discuss which rules or "norms" we might want to establish for our class based on classes (including our own) that have either been good or bad in the past and what made them so. Students create a T chart with the experience on one side and then a norm for it on the other.

Experience

Norm

I've had a class where all the students were always talking during the lesson.

Don't talk while someone else is talking.

I've had a boring online class because no one talked.

Participate with your camera, microphone, and chat box during class.

Once the groups have brainstormed, I give each student a Google Form that I call "The Norm Form" (Figure 9.7) where they can submit the norms they would like us to adopt in class. I export those responses to a Google Sheet and copy and paste each unique response onto a Google Slide "anchor chart" that is bookmarked to my browser.

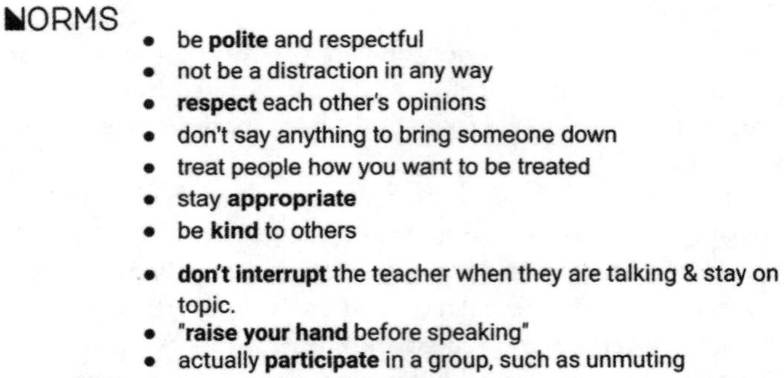

NORMS

- be **polite** and respectful
- not be a distraction in any way
- **respect** each other's opinions
- don't say anything to bring someone down
- treat people how you want to be treated
- stay **appropriate**
- be **kind** to others

- **don't interrupt** the teacher when they are talking & stay on topic.
- "**raise your hand** before speaking"
- actually **participate** in a group, such as unmuting

Figure 9.7: Student-created class norms.

From then on, at the start of each class (after our "mindful moment"), I show the students the norms they've set for themselves and ask them to quietly review them, reaffirming each day the behavior expectations they have for each other.

THE ONGOING "NORM FORM"

Although the primary intention of the "Norm Form" is for students to contribute the norms and expectations they have for each other, I also use it to create class culture and get student input for class.

After the initial norms have been contributed and agreed upon, I create a second version where I give students the option to:

- Contribute additional norms
- Propose and vote on a class name
- Suggest songs for me to play before class starts
- Upload images to use in our Google Classroom banner
- Propose community questions to ask at the start of class
- Suggest activities they'd like to do during class.

Aside from the class name, which we agree on at the start of the year, students have access to this second version of the "Norm Form" (posted on our Google Classroom) and they can contribute to our class culture throughout the year through music, art, and ideas.

I have the email notification setting turned on for this Google Form, so when a student requests a new song, I get the email notification and I try to play that song at the start of the next class period, or if they create a custom Google Classroom banner, I try to change it before the next class period. That way, students see that I am hearing and responding to their input.

In my experience, it seems to go a long way toward the students feeling like they have ownership and a sense of belonging in our class.

STAYING ENGAGED

Getting students interested and excited at the start of the school year is one thing, but keeping them engaged, particularly when they are learning remotely, is equally important.

Check-In

As I discuss in Chapter 2, Synchronous Learning, I check in with each student at the start of synchronous classes, typically by asking them how they are doing and asking a "community question." Beyond checking in during live classes, there are several other ways to check-in with students' well-being.

Google Forms or **Microsoft Forms** are fantastic tools for facilitating check-ins with students, whether they are quick "temperature checks," longer surveys, or collecting student input (see "The Norm Form" in the previous section). Here are a few different types of check-ins I conduct throughout the year:

- Beginning of the Year Survey

  At the start of each year, alongside the letter-writing activity, I give my students a form where I can collect information that might be helpful for me to know in order to better understand my students and their circumstances.

  What are you most nervous about this year?
  Describe where and when you usually do homework/your work at home.
  What is the biggest distraction when you are trying to do work?
  Do you live in a single home or travel between two or more places?
  What are your activities or responsibilities outside of school? (sports, hobbies, activities, chores, family, etc.)
  What is your favorite family tradition?
  Do you have access to the internet at home?
  Is there anything I should know about you physically? (health concerns, allergies, etc.?)
  Have you started thinking about future career and/or college goals? What are you thinking?
  Who helps you with schoolwork at home? How helpful are they?
  What was your favorite thing about your language arts class last year? Why?
  What things should I do as a teacher to help you do well this year?
  Is there anything else you would like to tell me about you?

- Community Check-In

  I facilitate a community check-in at the start of each synchronous class. Often these are in the style of a round-robin, or by entering responses in the chat box, but occasionally I'll ask students to complete their check-in through a Google Form, especially if I want to ask a question that students might not be as willing to share with the class.

  How are you feeling today on a scale of 1—10? Why?
  Community Question
  How do you feel you did on this certain assignment? Did you meet the expectations you have for yourself?

- Quarterly/Semester Class Survey

  At the end of each quarter or semester I give students the following Google Form survey to gauge how they feel the class is going as a whole. I show the data to the class on the first day of the start of the new quarter or semester to lead us in a conversation on what is going well/what we should continue to focus on and what could be improved/how we might do that.

Students in this class treat the teacher with respect.
(scale 1–10, agree/disagree)
The teacher in this class treats the students with respect.
(scale 1–10, agree/disagree)
I feel like I have a say in what we learn and how this class operates. (I feel like this is my class, and I have a lot of choice.)
(scale 1–10, agree/disagree)
My classmates behave the way my teacher wants them to.
(scale 1–10, agree/disagree)
My teacher uses effective methods for managing the classroom behavior.
(scale 1–10, agree/disagree)
Our class stays busy and doesn't waste time.
(scale 1–10, agree/disagree)
In class we learn a lot, almost every day.
(scale 1–10, agree/disagree)
This class is interesting to me and the lessons are fun and engaging.
(scale 1–10, agree/disagree)
The teacher cares about me and my learning.
(scale 1–10, agree/disagree)
I feel like I can trust my teacher and go to her if I ever need help.
(scale 1–10, agree/disagree)
I feel that the grades I receive are fair based on the work I did.
(scale 1–10, agree/disagree)
I feel safe and included in this classroom.
(scale 1–10, agree/disagree)
Please choose one of the questions above to elaborate on. Why did you give the score that you did?
What is your favorite thing you've done this year in class?
Is there something about this class, or something going on in class, that you wish Ms. Pass knew about?

The best thing about using Forms for checking in is the ability to save and export the data to spreadsheets and use it to refer to.

Mood meters are another fun, quick way to check in with students, either in class by projecting them to the whiteboard or sharing your screen or by inserting them into your Google Form check-in.

They are typically created based on a theme (cats, video game characters, etc.) and include 10 images each representing different moods. Every picture has a corresponding number, so you can ask your students how they are feeling today, and they can give you the number that represents the image and explain why.

Amanda Pace (@amandaapacee) has been very generously creating and sharing **mood meters** on Google Slides that educators can make a copy of for free! (See Figure 9.8.) But consider **donating to her classroom** in thanks.

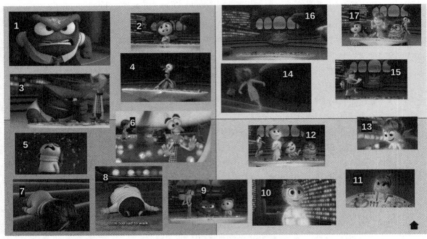

Figure 9.8: Epic mood meter by Amanda Pace.

Flipgrid is also a great tool for check-ins, especially on asynchronous days. Ask your students to record a short video at the start of asynchronous workdays, talking about how they are feeling, how their weekend was, and/or answer a community question. Students can watch each other's videos and leave comments when they make connections.

If you conduct individual check-ins with your students, either in person or virtually, you might consider using a system to track your communication and progress toward a goal. These might just be advisory/well-being check-ins, reading conferences, or project-based learning benchmarks.

Trello is my favorite progress monitoring site. On Trello, shown in Figure 9.9, you can create a project dashboard with steps in a process. Then, you create individual "cards" for each student, on which you can take notes or check off items in a list. These cards can be dragged and dropped and moved along the process, so when you look at your dashboard you have a great visual representation of where all your students are, and by clicking into the individual cards you can remind yourself of the details of each student's progress.

Figure 9.9: Trello.

The free version gives you access to 10 dashboards (which is more than enough for my classes). The premium versions provide unlimited access.

Virtual Spaces

However hard we try to structure our synchronous classes in a way that facilitates community building, the truth is that many connections are made through random encounters and conversations, which are difficult if your students aren't in a school building all (or any) of the time. The absence of lunchrooms or hallways, where they can chat and socialize, means students are missing out on valuable social and emotional learning. This is why it is incredibly important to establish safe, virtual spaces for students to meet and socialize.

At PSD Global Academy (PGA), we created several Google Meeting rooms that we called "lunchrooms," where students could join over their lunch hour when learning remotely, just to spend time with their friends. As teachers, we loosely monitored these rooms by popping in with our cameras and microphones turned off, to check in and make our presence known.

Eric Cross, a middle school science teacher in San Diego, recently introduced me to **Mozilla Hubs**, a virtual reality space similar to the mega-popular Nintendo game "Animal Crossing." With Mozilla Hubs, you can invite students to socialize in a space where they can move around and interact as avatars, which might be an interesting divergence from regular video conferencing. The major benefit to socializing in a space like Hubs is that multiple conversations can be happening within the same room, and the volume of the microphone is dependent on your proximity to another avatar. Students can huddle in groups and move between them to have conversations.

And, of course, don't forget to leverage the "home" or "stream" section of your LMS to create space for socialization (see Chapter 3, Asynchronous Learning).

Virtual Assemblies and Themed Days

School assemblies are one of the greatest ways to create a sense of all-school community and culture, and need not be forgone in a virtual environment.

Our school has conducted several very successful all-school themed days, assemblies, and fundraisers during the COVID school closure as a way to reestablish our school's community/culture and give students a break from the normal screen-based remote learning activities.

Victoria Wilson, a PGA middle school science teacher, designed our first all-school themed day for Earth Day. It started with a kickoff call over Google Meet, where our principal welcomed everyone and hyped up the students by allowing them to unmute in groups and cheer for their grade levels (for five seconds each).

Then, Wilson emceed the event dressed in a Captain Planet costume. She gave a brief history of Earth Day, and established the importance of celebrating the day and taking care of the environment. She then involved teachers from various grade levels and subjects by asking, "What are you doing today?"

Each of us was in a different outdoor space and modeled for the students how we would be celebrating Earth Day. For example, I was at my compost bin, another teacher was on a hike, while another was on her porch, making art from recycled materials.

From there, Wilson introduced a choice board of activities that students could engage in for the day (Figure 9.10). Most of the activities were not tech related. Students were asked to engage in, take pictures of, and post evidence of three activities on a Padlet Board by the end of the day.

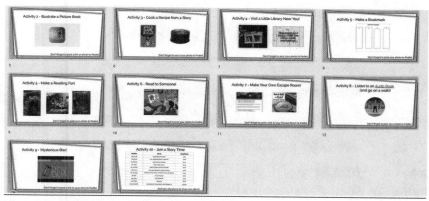

Figure 9.10: Read-a-Thon activity choice board.

Because of the success of Earth Day, we also decided to have an all-school **Read-a-Thon**. It was designed in the same way, with the all-school kickoff call that included a reading fort, a local author, and teachers dressed up as favorite book characters. Students also had a choice board of reading-related activities, as well as a reading competition that we tracked with a Google Form and a **Flippity Progress Tracker** (Figure 9.11).

Finally, we hosted our school's annual Fall Festival fundraiser event virtually in a similar fashion, by livestreaming a kickoff call to students, parents, and friends on YouTube. We then directed all attendees to a Google Site where the home page had a Google Form embedded with different options for helping our school with fundraising (box tops, Amazon Smile, King Soopers Loyalty, etc.). Every person who filled out the Form was entered into a raffle as were the participants of the game rooms, escape rooms, costume contest, and chili dinner. Each of these activities had their own page on the Google Site and either a link to a Google Meeting room (dance rooms, scary storytelling, escape/game rooms), shown in Figure 9.12, or a Padlet board for participants to post pictures (costume and chili contest). At the end of the night, we directed all participants back to the YouTube link and raffled off prizes for participants and contest winners.

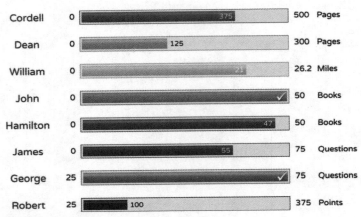

Figure 9.11: Flippity Progress Tracker.

Figure 9.12: Fall Festival virtual dance rooms.

It was a fantastic and fun way to keep our school's tradition alive.

Bring it back to the building

Although assemblies and events are always more fun in person, livestreaming events for students and parents who might not be able to attend is a great alternative. Many schools already livestream graduation ceremonies for out-of-town relatives, but this could also be extended to include school plays, concerts, sports events, and even classroom presentations.

Hosting them on a website (like Google Sites) could also provide the opportunity for parents to leave comments, make donations, or get additional information on school programs.

You may also consider holding an "Earth day," "Read-a-Thon," "field day," "game day," "world cultures day," "math in the real world day," or any other number of content-related themed days at the school building using virtual choice boards and even livestreaming the introduction to individual classrooms to save the time and effort of moving the entire school to the gym.

Spirit Week

PGA teachers Hannah McGrath and Stacy Denham spearhead frequent spirit weeks for PGA. They create a Google Slide document with the theme for each day of the week, and a link to a Padlet board, where students can post photos each day, as shown in Figures 9.13 and 9.14.

Gamify

Whether they are competitive or collaborative, content based or just for fun, I love playing games with my students. (Sometimes I wonder if I became a teacher so I could play games during the workday.)

Video Conferencing Icebreakers

I am often amazed at the creativity and ingenuity of humans. Since the push to remote learning because of COVID, I have seen so many amazing icebreakers that can be played over video conferencing, many of which I discovered from **@typebteacher**.

Bring it back to the building

If you have a spirit week at school, consider creating Padlet boards for each advisory or homeroom class and award prizes at the end of the week for the most spirited photos.

It's Spirit Week at PGA!

Post a selfie of your school spirit to each day's padlet and check back to see each other's school spirit. (Links are underlined.)

Monday: Pet/Stuffed Animal/Plant Selfie	Tuesday: Cozy Flannel/ Plaid Day	Wednesday: Crazy Hat and Sock Day	Thursday: PGA Gear/School Colors	Friday: Pajama Day
Share a pic of your favorite pet, stuffed animal, plant, or anything that brings you joy!	Post a selfie doing your school work in your comfiest flannel or plaid. Cozy vibes all around!	Now's the chance to share your love for all those wild and crazy accessories!	Dress in all your PGA gear/school colors! Post a pic to show off your amazing style.	Can't skip a crowd favorite! You know you're already in your pajamas, so show how you make them work for school too.

Figure 9.13: Virtual spirit week.

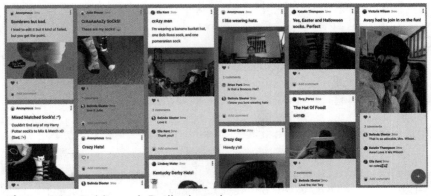

Figure 9.14: Spirit week Padlet board.

Pass the Pencil

For this, the teacher will need to have their video conferencing tool set up to view participants in grid view, then share their screen and stay on the video conferencing tool screen, so that all the participants see each other in the same orientation.

Done correctly, it should look like the Brady Bunch.

Each student should have their own pencil, then the teacher starts by "passing" the pencil off screen to one of the students, who "takes" the pencil from the same direction and then "passes" it on to the next.

This continues until the pencil has been "passed" to every student.

To make it more interesting, you could time yourselves to see how long it takes you, attempting to beat your time whenever you play.

Guess the Song

In this icebreaker, one participant turns on their camera, but keeps themselves on mute as they play a song and lip sync the lyrics (participants will not hear the song because the singer is muted).

All the other participants watch, trying to determine which song it is, and once they know, they join in on the lip syncing.

Once the original lip syncer determines that enough of the participants have guessed the song correctly, they can unmute their microphone, allowing the whole group to join in on the singing for the remainder of the song or for a few minutes until you switch.

60-Second Sketch

Make sure participants have a piece of paper and something to draw with. Then, give them a drawing prompt (cat, solar system, cat riding a convertible car through the solar system), then they have 60 seconds to draw (you could play music during this time), and when the 60 seconds are up, everyone holds their drawing up to the camera.

Follow the Leader

One person is the "observer" and temporarily leaves the room or closes their eyes while the teacher chooses a "leader." I write the leader's name on a piece of paper and hold it up to the camera so that everyone (but the "observer") can see.

When the observer returns, all the remaining participants are mimicking the leader's movements, and the observer has to try to guess and determine who the leader is.

Cameras On If

Give participants prompts that begin with "Turn your camera on if..." and have students respond based on whether their cameras are on or off. Some examples of prompts include:

Turn your cameras on if you've watched every season of "Stranger Things."
Turn your cameras on if you know what you are going to be for Halloween this year.
Turn your cameras on if you went to bed way too late last night. Show me with your fingers what time you went to sleep.

This is a great game to play if you are trying to encourage your students to turn on their cameras for class.

Simon Says

This version works just like the regular game, but instead of sitting down when you are "out," you turn your camera off.

Nonacademic Online Games

Outside of using games during class for content review, you could also consider offering an optional "Game Night" over Google Meet, just for fun.

Here are a few of my favorite digital games:

- **Brightful Meeting Games**—numerous games designed to be played over video conferencing including werewolf, draw it, and would you rather.
- **Bingo**—virtual bingo caller and cards.
- **Drawful 2**—a variety of Pictionary designed for video conferencing.
- **Codenames**—word-based guessing game.
- **Scattergories**—vocabulary game.
- **WordScatter**—word building game.
- **Wavelength**—partner guessing game.

- **Gartic.io**—digital variation of Pictionary
- **Find the Invisible Cow**—click around the screen until you hit the cow

Movie Night

I love movie days at school, but a remote movie day has the added benefit of no popcorn on the floor and no pausing the movie to ask the class to "keep it down" so that the students who want to watch can hear.

On Google Meet, you can now "Present a Tab," which will allow your students to hear the internal audio from your computer.

Then, students can use the chat box to chat about the movie if they want to, or they can exit the chat box and focus on the film. (I actually love seeing students' thoughts in the chat box as they watch movies over video conferencing.)

You can encourage your students to wear PJs, make popcorn, and bring snacks!

Check with your district about which movies you are licensed to show in your classrooms.

Virtual Field Trips

Virtual reality (VR) is still not as good as real life travel and experiences, but for today there are a couple of cool options that are better than nothing.

- **Roller Coaster**

  Theresa Hoover, fellow Google Certified Innovator and middle school band teacher, takes her students to an amusement park at the end of every school year. This year, in lieu of going in person, she met with her students over Google Meet and showed a roller coaster point of view (POV) video from YouTube (Figure 9.15). The whole class pretended to be on the ride, with their hands in the air, leaning with the turns in the video, and even yelling and screaming when the coaster dropped.

Riding "Surf Coaster" Roller Coaster at Sea Paradise in Japan! Front Seat 4K Onride POV

632,611 views · Oct 14, 2019   👍 3.6K   👎 352   ↗ SHARE   ≡+ SAVE   ···

Figure 9.15: Roller coaster POV video.

- Expeditions

    Google Expeditions is an app that provides hundreds of premade virtual tours from all over the world and even throughout time (see a Gladiator fight in "Ancient Rome," Figure 9.16). All your students need is the Expeditions app on their Chromebook device, tablet, or smartphone.

    Typically, tours are conducted from the classroom, where all the devices are linked to the same network, and therefore can be controlled by the teacher. With students learning remotely they will have to download and view the tour on their own.

    Luckily you can share a link to the exact tour you want your students to view.

    Students can "view" the tour in a panoramic view on their computers and don't need any special VR equipment. However, they could also "view in VR" for the full 360 experience if they build their own **VR headset** out of cardboard.

 No attribution
AR · 7 objects

Download to view or guide

The world of ancient Rome spanned a vast time period, from the 8th century BC to the 5th century AD, when the last of the Roman emperors was overthrown by Germanic invaders. Today, we're still fascinated by an empire that covered most of Europe, the Turkish Peninsula, the Middle East, and a wide swath of northern Africa. In this tour, we'll look at some artifacts from that lost world.

The World of Ancient Rome

Figure 9.16: Google Expeditions.

- Make your own VR Field Trip

  If you can't find the exact field trip you are looking for on Google Expeditions, consider creating your own! There are two DIY virtual reality tools that I like.

  - **Tour Creator** is another Google product, which allows you to use any Google Maps image or take your own pictures using an app called **Google Cardboard Camera**, and create a custom VR tour. Within these tours you can add multiple scenes, audio narration, and points of interest. Consider creating a tour of your school, city, or any other area that is specific to your needs.

- **CoSpaces** is another great VR tool. It differs from Google's tours in that the VR spaces you create are all animated — so the sky isn't even the limit!

Consider having students create their own VR tours on Tour Creator or CoSpaces. I have my 8th graders create dystopian landscapes on CoSpaces for our dystopian book club unit.

CONNECTING TO THE WORLD

More than ever, our world has learned the potential of virtual connection across distance. Whereas it might have been a big ask for someone to join our class as a guest speaker in the past, now many more people are familiar with video conferencing and willing to spend some time talking to students.

Use this as an opportunity to bring the community to your classroom. Ask local authors, artists, athletes, and leaders to join your virtual class and share their wisdom and experience.

Additionally, you could use a site like **Classroom Bridges** or **Empatico** to find other teachers and classrooms around the country or world to connect with to share cultural experiences or to create genuine audiences for sharing final projects.

Flipgrid also has a section of their website called "Gridpals" where you can find other classrooms to connect with for a Flipgrid conversation.

You'll be surprised at how many people say yes. All you have to do is ask!

RESOURCES

Items in **bold** in the text are listed here in the Resources. Direct access to all the following resources is available at https://hybridteacherresource.com and on this book's page on www.wiley.com.

Dwyer, K., Bingham, S. G., Carlson, R. E. et al. (2004). Communication and connectedness in the classroom: Development of the connected classroom climate inventory. *Communication Research Reports* 21 (3): 268–272.

Applied Digital Skills—https://applieddigitalskills.withgoogle.com/s/en/home

Liz Galarza uses dialogue journals—https://www.cultofpedagogy.com/dialogue-journals/

Letter Writing Slide Deck—https://docs.google.com/presentation/d/1mIoMhY2PvsHcNwGw4tD9tdstTqjio2ZebV5gQ2W7PAY/edit?usp=sharing

Create a Scrapbook Page—https://applieddigitalskills.withgoogle.com/c/middle-and-high-school/en/create-a-scrapbook/overview.html

Applied Digital Skills lesson—https://applieddigitalskills.withgoogle.com/c/middle-and-high-school/en/build-a-portfolio-with-google-sites/overview.html

Google Sites tutorials—https://www.youtube.com/results?search_query=new+google+sites+tutorial

Google Site template—https://drive.google.com/drive/folders/1g9VkgcNx1ti-_QJB-jU7bAL_GbtUOfS8?usp=sharing

Google Drawing Template—https://docs.google.com/drawings/d/1Y4v6bHM5fgT38-UqZEqdhksuxkyXtfhADzHdHDqgj1I/copy?usp=sharing

Vocaroo—https://vocaroo.com

Stephanie Rothstein's Twitter—https://twitter.com/Steph_EdTech

"Can We Talk: Personality, Teams, Conversation, and Feedback"—https://www.youtube.com/watch?v=RAL1M3pVt8M

Google Jamboard—https://jamboard.google.com

Create a guessing game—https://applieddigitalskills.withgoogle.com/c/middle-and-high-school/en/create-a-guessing-game/overview.html

Quizizz—https://quizizz.com

Kahoot—https://kahoot.com

Gimkit—https://www.gimkit.com

Classmate Trivia Form—https://docs.google.com/
forms/d/1VZ3bIFqLu2KApxtOG1qvD-vCmQNzy3FG1VcvOGKn9eg/
copy?usp=sharing

Padlet—http://padlet.com

Flipgrid—https://info.flipgrid.com

List of Community Building Questions—https://blog.flipgrid.com/
news/selbongi

Virtual Dice—https://www.google.com/search?q=virtual+dice&rlz=1CAG
ZLV_enUS871US871&oq=virtual+dic&aqs=chrome.0.0l2j69i57j0l5.2162j0j1&s
ourceid=chrome&ie=UTF-8

Google Forms—https://www.google.com/forms/about/

Microsoft Forms—https://forms.office.com

Mood Meters—https://docs.google.com/presentation/d/1kBwhuPI-kb3e
mYpN9RqQ5QviJuUFx7jH_qPfXBQoN6w/edit#slide=id.g93ad86efec_0_0

Amanda Pace Donation—https://cash.app/$amandaapacee

Eric Cross' Twitter—https://twitter.com/sdteaching

Mozilla Hubs—https://hubs.mozilla.com/#/

Read-a-Thon—https://docs.google.com/presentation/d/1Kg-
8I8UJDpVuCqhKwjZ8mgVmwYm6dM4f87J82OTAdp8/edit?usp=sharing

Flippity Progress Tracker—https://flippity.net/ProgressIndicator.htm

Type B Teacher TikTok—https://www.tiktok.com/@typebteacher

Brightful Meeting Games—https://www.brightful.me/play/#fast_
paced_games

Bingo—https://www.bingomaker.com/web-app/

Drawful 2—https://www.jackboxgames.com/drawful-two/

Codenames—https://www.horsepaste.com

Scattergories—https://scattergoriesonline.net

WordScatter—http://www.wordscatter.com

Wavelength—https://longwave.web.app

Gartic.io—https://gartic.io

Find the Invisible Cow—https://findtheinvisiblecow.com

Roller Coaster—https://www.youtube.com/
watch?v=KFuHikdkBXw&feature=emb_logo

How to Build a VR Headset—https://www.youtube.com/
watch?v=8qNmRi-gNqE

Tour Creator—https://arvr.google.com/tourcreator/

Google Cardboard Camera—https://support.google.com/cardboard/
answer/6329800?co=GENIE.Platform%3DAndroid&hl=en

CoSpaces—https://cospaces.io/edu/

Classroom Bridges—https://www.classroombridges.com

Empatico—https://empatico.org

Chapter 10
Attendance and Assessment

There is no failure. Only feedback.

—Robert Allen

Whether you are teaching synchronously, asynchronously, in a brick-and-mortar classroom or online only, you'll need to assess student understanding in order to identify what is working and for whom.

Taking attendance and monitoring student progress are considerably easier in a brick-and-mortar classroom, so the following advice is directed at remote learning models.

ATTENDANCE

Before you jump into assessment of content knowledge, you might first consider your system for tracking who is engaging in the work in the first place.

Synchronous Attendance

Taking attendance for synchronous learning is a little more straightforward. If you are with students in the classroom, it's a simple matter of tracking who is physically present.

For online synchronous learning, you could go one of two routes. First, you could take attendance based purely on whether the student logs in to the virtual class. If their avatar is there, they are there. There are currently a number of tools to make this easier on **video conferencing software.**

Google Meet

In Google Meet, if you are recording your session (which I highly recommend), the transcript from the chat box will be saved as a Google Doc alongside your video in your Drive.

I ask my students to simply type "here" into the chat box once we start the class so I can go back later and take attendance on the Google Doc.

Google Meet also now sends you a spreadsheet of meeting data after the video conference has ended, including the names of all the participants and the amount of time they spent in the meeting.

If you are not recording meetings, there are also a number of Google Chrome Extensions that automatically take attendance for you within Google Meet:

- **Google Meet Attendance**
- **Google Meet Attendance Collector**
- Meet Attendance

Microsoft Teams

In Microsoft Teams you can download a list of attendees for any meeting. One nice feature in Teams is the ability to rejoin a meeting and download the list retroactively after you've finished a class.

Simply click on the "participants" icon and the "download" icon to download your list of participants during that session.

Zoom

In Zoom, you can track attendance based on your usage reports.

To track attendance in Zoom simply go to "reports," "usage," and select the date and time range for that class. You should then see a detailed list of your attendees for that session, including the exact times they logged on, off, and the duration of their attendance.

Knowing which students signed in to your online class is valuable information. It tells you that the student had a device, internet access, and made the effort to get online for class. However, you might consider requiring a little more than simply logging on for attendance or participation points.

I have had students who log in to Google Meet, then turn their camera off and leave to do other things. I know this because they become entirely unresponsive and do not participate in class activities. They are also often the last ones in Meet, because they aren't paying attention to when the class ends in time to exit. I ask myself, should this student really be marked "present" for that day's online class?

One strategy we use at PGA is to mark attendance on a scale, rather than being "present" or "absent." Instead, we give students a percentage for their attendance. Most students are 100% present, but the student who logs on but doesn't participate might be marked only 50% present for that day.

This system also helps our administrative team identify which students are scoring lowest in attendance, so they can reach out to those families to provide additional support.

Asynchronous Attendance

Similar to synchronous attendance, it is important to understand which students are logging in on a daily basis for their asynchronous work, in order to provide support and interventions to those students who aren't engaging from home.

Depending on the platform and systems your district is using, you will have different data on what your student is doing from home.

Google Classroom

Although Google Classroom doesn't track when a student logs on or how long they spend on the platform in general; anytime a student engages in anything (writes a comment, works on an assignment in a Google Doc) that activity will be time stamped, so you will have some basic idea of what they are doing and when.

Figure 10.1: Google Classroom attendance question.

You might also consider **posting a Google Classroom Question** each day of the week for attendance, shown in Figure 10.1.

These questions can be scheduled to automatically post every morning.

Again, this won't tell you whether your students actually completed their work for the day or how long they worked, but it will show you that they had access and made the effort to get online.

Sometimes I am tempted to make an attendance question more involved (ask a community or comprehension question) rather than simply clicking a button. But I would urge you to keep it as simple as possible. You will still be posting content for them in their classwork for the day, and you can always build community in the Stream, but you don't want to lose your attendance data because a student couldn't think of an answer.

Keep it simple.

You might also consider posting a Google Form for daily attendance. The benefit of this is you can use the same Form every day without needing to change it. At the end of the week you can download all the responses to a Google Sheet and sort by the time stamp to see which students logged on each day. The downside? It would require a tiny bit more work on the student's end—a couple more buttons to push and information to input—which might mean students are less likely to do it.

Schoology

One of the benefits of using a subscription learning management system (LMS) like Schoology is the access to usage analytics.

Within Schoology you have the ability to pull a report on which students accessed the platform that day and how long they spent there.

Simply click "tools," "usage analytics," and customize your date and time range to determine your asynchronous attendance for that day.

Canvas

One of the benefits of using a subscription LMS like Canvas is the ability to access reports.

Within Canvas you have the ability to pull a report on each student and view whether they accessed the platform that day and how long they spent there.

Click the "people" tab and once you select an individual student you will see an option to run an "access report" to determine their attendance for the day.

Once you have an attendance routine for asynchronous learning days, you'll need to ask yourself the same question I discussed in the synchronous attendance section earlier in this section—Is logging in enough? Or do students need to engage in their actual work to receive attendance credit or participation points for the day?

At PGA we give students a percentage for daily attendance. I give students 50% attendance for simply logging on and clicking "here." From there I quickly assess who completed their work that day for the rest of the score. Even if I don't have time to fully grade or give feedback on work, I'll scan through the entire class and just look for students who didn't complete anything or only partially completed work for that day in order to keep track of attendance.

During the times when PGA moved to 100% online learning in response to COVID, I doubled my effort to capture attendance (or perhaps it should be called "engagement data") every day. I report the average weekly attendance for each student to the administration, who meets to determine how they will be contacting and supporting families who are at the lowest engagement levels and highest risk.

ASSESSMENT

Key Terms

Formative Assessment	Assessment done during the learning process to inform how the teacher should modify future learning experiences.
Summative Assessment	An assessment done at the end of a unit to gauge a student's understanding.

We should start by addressing the big elephant in the room when it comes to assessing students who are learning remotely: Google.

More specifically, students' ability to use Google to search for answers.

Although often our friend, Google can be frustrating for teachers who are trying to genuinely assess student understanding in a remote learning environment.

When we are in the classroom, it is much easier to determine whether students are actually doing their work or if they are looking up answers online. Even my students who are super fast and sneaky at hiding windows can't get much Googling accomplished during an assessment when I am walking through the room monitoring their screens. In a classroom, I can ensure that the majority of the time spent on assessment is genuine.

If you are teaching in a hybrid model, where you see students for part of the week, my best advice is to **save summative assessments for in-person days.**

But what if we are in a scenario that requires remote-only learning? Or what about students who can't come to school? When students are home, how can we guarantee that they aren't looking up every single answer online?

The short answer is: we can't.

There are tools I will discuss later to help with security and monitoring student work, but I've never found it very productive to resist a reality. I'd rather spend my time and energy working with it.

In order to work with the system we have, consider if you can create:

- A grading system where students don't feel the need to cheat

- A culture and community where students don't want to cheat

- Assessments where students are encouraged to use their resources to seek information

- Alternative assessments where students are producing original thoughts and products that they won't be able to find online

Can You Create a Grading System Where Students Don't Feel the Need to Cheat?

Let's consider why students feel the need to cheat in the first place. More often than not, it is the pressure to get a good grade. I think we've put so much emphasis on grades in our society that it has become a form of classroom currency; trading points for tissue boxes and offering extra credit for additional work as if it were overtime pay. In a system like this, what message are we sending our students? What is most important? The learning? Or the grade?

Many students (my younger self included) learn how the grading system works and game it to get the necessary points, rather than focusing on deep learning and understanding of the content. When we turn our education system into a game, some students will do anything to win—including cheat.

But when we shift the focus back on learning and eliminate or reduce the importance of the grade, students have less incentive to cheat.

One way to do this is to offer **unlimited redos and revisions on work**.

I've been offering this to my students for the past five years with great success. I share this policy with my students at the beginning of the year (and remind them of it before any major assessment or project is due). I emphasize that they are in complete control of their grade; anything they'd like to score better on, they can continue to redo until they get the score they want. That way, there is no reason to cheat or plagiarize. The emphasis is on the learning rather than the grade.

When I first considered implementing this policy I had three main concerns:

1. Would I have an unmanageable increase in grading if students are continuing to redo or revise work?

2. Would students put less effort into the original work because they know they can redo it?

3. Would every student have 100% in my class?

The answer to all of those questions is no. I find that students don't *want* to redo work, so they put the same effort into their first attempt as they would their only attempt. There are one or two students in every class who redo everything to get to 100%, but most don't feel that need for perfection; and although I do regrade plenty of work, it is typically pretty quick because I know exactly what I am looking for based on the feedback I gave initially.

If you think about it, regrading revised work is a whole lot easier than creating and grading extra credit assignments.

Another option to consider is going completely gradeless in your classroom. Our PGA High School English team is gradeless and have recommended Sarah Zerwin's book *Point-Less: An English Teacher's Guide to More Meaningful Grading*.

If dismantling grading feels a little radical to you, keep in mind most countries don't grade like we do in the United States. When I taught in England I gave feedback on almost every piece of work a student did but almost never assigned a grade for it. The few grades they did receive were on summative assignments and assessments. This system makes a lot more sense to me, to focus on the feedback rather than the score.

Can You Create a Culture and Community Where Students Don't Want to Cheat?

In addition to creating a system where students have less incentive to cheat because they don't feel the pressure for their grade, I also try to develop a culture in which students don't want to.

As you know, I start with the "why?"

Elementary students are fond of asking "why?"—"Why are we learning this?" or "Why does this matter?" Not only do I think this is an excellent question, I think it is essential to answer this question for everything we teach. And if you can't give an answer to "why are we learning this?" you might spend some time reflecting on it to ensure your teaching is meaningful.

As students age through the school system, however, they tend to ask "why?" less and less often, so I recommend bringing it up yourself.

One of the first lessons I do every school year is "Why English Matters." In that lesson I do my best to persuade students that not just getting a good grade, but really learning and retaining the skills I teach will be essential to their future success. We look at data that correlate literacy rates to income, funny spelling mistakes in public places, and a heartwarming video on the power of communication.

Then, I try to give my students a brief "why this matters" for everything unit and tie it to how it might help them in their futures.

Understanding who your students are and what their hopes are for the future is essential in doing this. Many of my students aspire to YouTube fame, so turning our instructional writing unit into creating YouTube videos helps them understand how they can apply the skills they are learning in school to the real world.

I also think the "what" is important when it comes to assessment.

Before any major project or assessment I very clearly explain exactly what the expectations are. It might sound obvious, but sometimes when there is a "gray area" and the expectations haven't been made crystal clear, students who wouldn't typically cheat drift into that gray area.

After so many instances of giving our students assignments over the years, I think we, as teachers, assume the expectations are obvious and students "should know" them; but it never hurts to take that little bit of time to clarify.

For example, this is what I typically say before the start of every in-class assessment:

> "I expect this work to be done entirely on your own, and for you to stay in the assessment window throughout the entirety of the exam without going to any other tabs or windows to look for answers on Google, Classroom, or your notes. You cannot talk to anyone else during the exam, even if the person behind you is kicking your chair and you need to ask them to stop. Raise your hand and I'll come over, because whispering sounds like cheating, even if it isn't. Similarly, if you are looking around the room, that can look like you are trying to see someone else's screen. If you need an eye break you can put your head down on your desk or look up at the ceiling."

I also include an academic honesty agreement section to the beginning of every assessment that students read and agree to, shown in Figure 10.2.

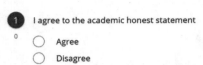

Academic Honesty

I commit to working on this assessment on my own, without help from any other person, website, book, or resource.

The knowledge shown on this assessment is a true reflection on what I currently know.

If I don't do as well as I'd like, I know that I can keep learning and redo the assessment later on.

1   I agree to the academic honest statement
0   ○   Agree
    ○   Disagree

Figure 10.2: Academic honesty agreement.

Giving those clear boundaries will force students into the position of explicitly and knowingly choosing to cheat; but, again, when the expectations are laid out in front of them like that, most choose not to.

Can You Create Assessments Where Students Are Encouraged to Use Their Resources to Seek Information?

Even if your classroom systems and cultures are established to encourage students not to cheat, the opportunity is always there. Again, I'll always choose to work with a reality rather than against it.

Our reality is we have nearly limitless and immediate access to information at our fingertips.

(Remember when our math teachers told us we wouldn't be carrying around calculators in our pockets when we grew up?)

Lesson Plans

- Instead of having students memorize a math equation, can you set a problem where they have to figure out the best equation to use? And find the resources to help them solve the problem?

- Instead of memorizing facts about a time period, can we have students use their research skills to build a custom timeline?

- Instead of memorizing vocabulary, can we ask students to research the etymology of a word and then create an entirely new vocabulary word using the same foundation?

So how can we use this to our advantage? Can we create assessments where being able to effectively seek out information is one of the skills we are assessing our students on? After all, understanding a topic is essential to effectively researching it.

Lesson Plans

Consider allowing students to use their notes and resources to create their own test or quiz. Using a Google Form, they can write one question for each piece of content knowledge, followed by one correct and three incorrect answers. Then, pair up students to take and grade each other's exams.

There is an Applied Digital Skills lesson to help students learn how to **design a quiz in Google Forms**.

Additionally, having students create their own exams or quiz questions is a great way to assess their understanding. Just think about how much of an expert you became in your content area within the first few years of teaching it. Teaching is the best way to learn.

Can You Create Assessments Where Students Are Producing Original Thoughts and Products That They Won't Be Able to Find Online?

This brings us to an entirely different way of looking at assessment. If you are ready to try something a little new, consider one of the following options:

- Written assessments

  When we ask our students to explain their thinking, it forces them to fully understand the process.

  As an English teacher, written assessments are a given, and with plenty of plagiarism checkers on the market (including **EasyBib**, **Grammarly**, and **Google Classroom Originality Reports**) it is pretty easy to assess whether the writing has been done by your students.

  Even if you are not an English teacher, there is no reason why a student wouldn't be able to write out their thinking process for a math equation or explain how a scientific process works.

- Concept Maps

  Although writing is an important skill, and a great way to assess understanding, it benefits the students who are stronger in their writing abilities.

  A similar approach would be to ask students to create a concept map, or other visual representation that demonstrates their understanding (Figure 10.3).

  Mind Mapping and **Sketchnoting** are two options for concept mapping. You may even consider giving students the choice between completing a written or visual response.

- Discussion-Based Assessment

  Similar to written assessment, discussion-based assessment (DBA) is a great way to determine the depth of a student's understanding. When

Figure 10.3: Example of visual note-taking.

you have to explain something out loud, you need to understand it pretty well.

Consider scheduling one-on-one or small-group discussions with your students over video conferencing; use the conversation that follows as your formal assessment.

If you are trying to schedule a large number of students for DBA, consider using a scheduling assistant like **Sign Up Genius** or using **Google Calendar Appointment Slots** to have your students sign up for sessions.

DBA can be nerve racking for some students, so you might give them a set of questions they can be expected to answer beforehand. Even letting students lead the discussion can help them feel more comfortable.

Lesson Plans

Subject/topic: Any

Although DBA is typically used as a summative assessment, it can also be used as a preassessment to gauge a student's understanding before a unit.

Brook Bess of Florida Virtual School and Jessica Carter of FLVS Global offer a great DBA based lesson: Students film a **Flipgrid** video before a unit to explain what they know about the topic. Then, the students respond to their OWN video after the unit, correcting any misconceptions they originally had and elaborating with new knowledge they've gained.

- Presentations/Become the Teacher

  I also like assigning students or student groups a topic to teach the class as a part of an end-of-unit review. I assess their understanding of the topic based on how they put their presentation and lesson together.

  I ask the students to do a short lesson/explanation, then an activity with the class for everyone to practice the material. Students get to make their own Kahoot, worksheets, and Pear Decks for the class. They get the power to be the teacher, and it is always fun to see what they do.

  This could be easily adapted to an online environment by either asking students to present their lessons over Google Meet or having them create asynchronous lessons for each other.

- Project-Based Learning

  As I mentioned earlier, project-based learning is a great experience for a hybrid model, particularly on asynchronous learning days.

  But if you are engaging in project-based learning, it's not as easy to glance at a worksheet or essay to gauge student understanding. Consider asking students to summarize what they did each day in a Google Classroom Question or Google Form, then use that for assessment and attendance data.

If you are really feeling creative, you could ask students to upload a photo of their progress to a Google Form, Padlet, or Google Slide, or schedule a video call and ask students to talk you through their process.

Incentive and Reward

There is debate in the pedagogical world about whether positive reinforcement is actually positive (extrinsic vs intrinsic motivations specifically), but at this stage in my career, I am never too far from a bag of candy to provide positive reinforcement for my students.

Here are a couple other extrinsic motivators to consider for teaching remotely.

- Mailing Prizes

  Stacy Denham, PGA teacher, interventionist, and middle school team lead, used our PTO budget to deliver "Tubs O' Love" (Figure 10.4) to each staff member on the middle school team this past spring.

  Within the box was an abundance of cool stickers, cards, envelopes, stamps, and return address labels.

  When we engage in 100% remote learning, I mail stickers to students as prizes, rewards, and positive reinforcement. I choose about five students per live-class day to mail stickers to, and it becomes a quick and easy routine that is fun and exciting for students.

  With large class sizes, it's difficult to regularly send mail to an entire class (or classes) of students, which is one reason I love raffles so much.

  Throughout a lesson, week, or unit, students can earn "raffle tickets" as positive reinforcement, then at the end of the lesson/week/unit, I use **Flippity Random Name Picker** or **Random Name Picker** and enter each student's name based on the number of "tickets" they have. Sometimes I'll spin the wheel for prizes during a live, synchronous class, and sometimes I screen record a video of it and post it to our Google Classroom stream.

- Postcard Apps

  Similar to mailing prizes, but a little more high tech, you could consider using a postcard app, such as **TouchNote** or **Felt**, that allows you to

Figure 10.4: Tub O' Love.

create a custom card on their app (including using your own images and handwritten notes), and they will mail the postcard for you.

Each app has both monthly subscriptions or charges by the individual postcards sent.

One other benefit to using an app like this is that postcards can be scheduled, which is great for sending your students birthday cards.

- Digital Badges

  If mailing stickers is cost or time prohibitive, consider the virtual equivalent. Host a space (Google Slides or Site) where students can earn a digital badge/sticker for winning a Kahoot for perfect attendance. You can create these badges quickly and easily with shapes and images in a Google Drawing and upload it to your students' "badge page" on Slides or Sites.

  I think digital badges could be a great alternative to offering extra credit as classroom currency for things like attendance and participation. Let the grade reflect student content knowledge, and the badges reflect everything else. (See Figure 10.5.)

Figure 10.5: Digital badges.

If you choose to use this method, be sure you dedicate time to hyping it up. Make sure the badges are visible to students (post them to your Google Classroom Stream and Banner) and celebrate "badging ceremonies" to get enough buy-in from students so that the badges become meaningful.

Security Tools and Strategies

At this point I hope you feel confident in building a system, culture, and curriculum in which you can accurately assess and reward student understanding, whether they are in class or working remotely.

Still, there are a couple of extra security measures you can put in place if you want to.

The first option is to use a program like **GoGuardian** or **Hāpara** that can track what a student is doing on a managed device. Basically you can spy on your students' computer screens from anywhere. (I use the word "spy" intentionally, because that's exactly how students feel about it.) I use tools like these very sparingly because I think relationships need to be founded on trust. If I am going to use them, I'll always show my students exactly what I can see and warn them in advance that I'll be using it.

If you are giving a unit exam, you could be monitoring all your students' screens on GoGuardian to make sure they are only on the exam and not venturing elsewhere on the web to seek answers.

This feature is nice for the classroom because you can sit at your desk and monitor student devices as well as their physical behavior to ensure they aren't asking for answers or looking on their phones. But what if all the students are working from home? How can we be sure they aren't looking at their phones? Or talking to an older sibling?

We also can't use parents or guardians to monitor their students while they take an assessment because we can't be sure all students are getting equal and fair treatment from their parents or guardians.

My advice is this: If you are teaching in a hybrid model where students are coming to school at least once a week and you really want to give a traditional summative assessment, do so when the students are on campus.

If you need to deliver an assessment online, ask them to schedule a time to join you on Google Meet and either ask them to share their screen or tell them you will be monitoring their work on GoGuardian, clearly outline the expectations, and (hopefully) remind them that they'll be able to redo or revise the work later if they are unhappy with their score.

Bring it back to the building

EDTECH ASSESSMENT TOOLS

Regardless of where you are giving an assessment, or what style you choose, here are a few of my favorite online assessment tools:

- **Google Forms**—Quick, easy, versatile, and scores can be imported to Google Classroom (GC) Gradebook
- **GoFormative**—Create assessments and view responses in real time
- **Quizziz**—Fast-paced, review-style game. View data after as formative assessment
- **Pear Deck**—Interactive Slides questions for formative assessment during lessons
- **Edpuzzle**—Interactive video questions for comprehension checks
- **Peer Grade**—Anonymous peer feedback and grading platform
- **Google Classroom Rubrics**—Attach rubrics to GC assignments to self-assessment
- **Google Classroom Originality Reports**—Google Classroom's plagiarism checker
- **Turn It In**—Popular online plagiarism checker
- **Word Wall**—Numerous review style games including a Pac-Man knockoff, and Whack-a-mole

RESOURCES

Items in **bold** in the text are listed here in the Resources. Direct access to all the following resources is available at https://hybridteacherresource.com and on this book's page on www.wiley.com.

Google Meet Attendance—https://chrome.google.com/webstore/search/Google%20Meet%20Attendance

Google Meet Attendance Collector—https://chrome.google.com/webstore/search/Google%20Meet%20Attendance%20collector

Post announcements to your students—https://support.google.com/edu/classroom/answer/6020270?co=GENIE.Platform%3DDesktop&hl=en

Point-Less: An English Teacher's Guide to More Meaningful Grading by Sarah Zerwin—https://www.heinemann.com/products/e10951.aspx

Design a quiz in Google Forms—https://applieddigitalskills.withgoogle.com/c/middle-and-high-school/en/create-quizzes-in-google-forms/overview.html

EasyBib—https://www.easybib.com/grammar-and-plagiarism/

Grammarly—https://www.grammarly.com/plagiarism-checker

Google Classroom Originality Reports—https://support.google.com/edu/classroom/answer/9335816?hl=en

Mind Mapping—https://www.mindmapping.com

Sketchnoting—https://sylviaduckworth.com/sketchnotefever/

Sign Up Genius—https://www.signupgenius.com

Google Calendar Appointment Slots—https://support.google.com/calendar/answer/190998?co=GENIE.Platform%3DDesktop&hl=en

Flipgrid—https://info.flipgrid.com

Flippity Random Name Picker—https://www.flippity.net/Random-NamePicker.htm

Random Name Picker—https://www.classtools.net/random-name-picker/

TouchNote—https://touchnote.com/us/

Felt—https://www.feltapp.com

GoGuardian—https://www.goguardian.com

Hāpara—https://hapara.com

Google Forms—https://www.google.com/forms/about/

GoFormative—https://goformative.com

Quizizz—https://quizizz.com

Pear Deck—https://www.peardeck.com

Edpuzzle—https://edpuzzle.com

PeerGrade—https://www.peergrade.io

Google Classroom Rubrics—https://support.google.com/edu/classroom/answer/9335069?co=GENIE.Platform%3DAndroid&hl=en

Turn It In—https://www.turnitin.com

Word Wall—https://wordwall.net

Chapter 11
Little Learners

Early childhood education is the key to the betterment of society.
—Maria Montessori

HYBRID FOR LITTLE LEARNERS

Although much of what I say in this book applies to learners of all ages, I realize that our littlest learners (preK-2) tend to need more adaptations and accommodations.

Emma Chitters teaches K-2 at the International School of Luxembourg (ISL). Her school switched to remote learning in March of 2020, but reopened in a hybrid model from May through July of that year.

Her first tip for K-2 teachers is to use **Seesaw** as your learning management system (LMS).

Seesaw is a digital app that acts as a student portfolio of learning. It has thrived in the elementary education space for its incredibly simple and intuitive tools that allow students to video and voice record, write, type, and draw. Student work is also easily viewable by parents and closely monitored by teachers.

Chitters and her colleagues had been using Seesaw (see Figure 11.1) as their LMS even before the pandemic, primarily as a learning center and as a way to demonstrate the learning their students were doing at school with their families. Seesaw was used as a learning portfolio for students to be able to look back and reflect on work they had previously done. Students would use their Seesaw portfolios during "parent–teacher conferences" to lead the discussion on what they were learning (yes, K-2 students!)

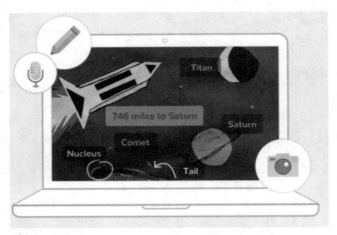

Figure 11.1: Seesaw.

When ISL went entirely remote in March 2020, they relied on Seesaw to deliver asynchronous learning experiences for students to complete from home. Chitters used Seesaw to post daily morning messages for her students (including the instructions for the day, and a warm-up activity like yoga), then self-directed activities. She found the activities that were most successful were the ones her students could do with the most independence. Although she thought making pancakes would be a popular activity, the reliance on parent participation meant a lot of students would not get it done. Simple coloring pages were much more successful because her students could navigate the work themselves.

She also found it was essential to communicate to parents the pedagogical importance of the activities she was assigning and to articulate how the activities met academic standards. For example, if she were to assign a recycled art activity to students, parents often wouldn't help facilitate the activity without understanding how the process (designing, repurposing, cutting, and explaining their thought process) was educational. She broke down each activity for them in order to "get that buy-in from parents."

During the 100% remote learning phase, Chitters emphasized that listening to parents' feedback is the best tool to inform how they progressed in their teaching and learning models. One piece of feedback from parents was the desire for students to meet synchronously with teachers over a video conferencing tool in order to maintain relationships between teacher and student and classmates.

Therefore, ISL started to conduct synchronous learning over Google Meet. Chitters acknowledged it could sometimes be a challenge to keep everyone's attention. Setting the norms and expectations was critical for her little learners as well and included teaching them how to mute and unmute their microphones (using visual signs as cues), physically raise their hands when they wanted to speak, then wait until they were called on to unmute themselves.

Read alouds and 20 questions were two activities she found particularly successful over Google Meet.

Luxembourg was in the unique situation of controlling the virus relatively quickly, and they were able to return to the classroom in May 2020. ISL used an A/B group hybrid model, where the students alternated on-campus vs remote learning every other week (read more about COVID response hybrid models in The Administrators' Appendix).

Their safety measures for students returning to campus started with having students wait to enter the building spaced six feet apart (marked with caution tape), then a teacher came to collect them and walked them past an automatic temperature scanning kiosk, before escorting them to their classrooms to wash their hands and sit in socially distanced boxes taped out on the floor. Each student also had their own desk and set of individual supplies.

The staff at ISL recognized that returning to school could be scary for some students and families and worked hard to make sure it was a positive and exciting experience by playing fun music for students as they waited to be escorted through the building, creating a balloon arch around the entryway of the building, and even, as shown in Figure 11.2, dressing their temperature scanning kiosk up like minions from Despicable Me (can you find the scanner?)

Figure 11.2: Minion temperature scanning kiosks.

In this hybrid model, the students who were spending their week on campus would start off with studio time, a play-based learning model, where students could use any of their individual materials to build or create anything they wanted. Often, Chitters would also create special spaces in the room that the students could visit individually to use classroom material (blocks, for example). In this case, she notes how helpful it was for her to have a teaching assistant in the room to help clean each "special space" between each user.

With the exception of outdoor time, the students stayed in their classroom for the entire day, including lunch and "extracurriculars" like art and physical education; in which case the specialist teacher would come to their room.

Chitters notes that the education they were providing in this hybrid model was much more play based than they are typically used to, with the express goal of encouraging as much socialization as possible. Part of that socialization was connecting with the students who were spending their week at home.

Each day in the classroom the students would have Seesaw time, where they would use classroom iPads (sanitized) to comment on the work their classmates were posting from home. As I discussed in Chapter 10 in the section "Asynchronous Discussion," it is important to structure how students have discussions online and littler learners are no different. One discussion model Chitters uses is "Glow and Grow," where her students comment on one thing they really like (the "glow") and one thing they think their classmate can improve upon (the "grow").

In this hybrid model, the students who were spending their week learning remotely from home had asynchronous activities posted for them in Seesaw (just like during remote learning), with the addition of connecting with the students who were in the classroom that day.

Not only were their classmates commenting on their asynchronous work, but Chitters would post videos from the activities they were doing in the classroom. One example is when her students (in the classroom) learned a TikTok dance during a brain break, she filmed the experience, posted it on Seesaw, and asked the students at home to watch, follow along, and post their own video of the TikTok dance.

Additionally, twice a week the whole class had Google Meets where the students in the classroom would be on Meet together, and each student at home would join the Meet individually. It was a way for them to have a quick check-in, share out, or dance party all together before they started their day. Upon reflection, Chitters said she would have liked to do one every morning, because it was such a great way to connect.

Although ISL had great plans and systems in place, Chitters acknowledges the difficulty of engaging the students who were learning from home.

You can read more about Chitters' experience living in Luxembourg on her **blog**.

ADDITIONAL ELEMENTARY IDEAS

Here are a few additional resources you might consider if you are implementing hybrid, remote, or blended learning for elementary aged students.

- Elementary teacher **Lisa Ann** (@terifficteaching) came up with a brilliant strategy for engaging her young students during remote, synchronous teaching. She had a sheet of star stickers next to her computer. Every time her students answered a question correctly, she put a star sticker on her face. Her students loved it and were motivated to keep answering correctly. By the end of the lesson, her face was covered in stars.

- **Novel Effect** is a spectacular sound effect app for story time. When you download the app, you can choose from hundreds of books (ideally you already have the book or can borrow it digitally from your local library). Once you start reading, their technology recognizes the words you are saying and provides music and sound effects to accompany that part of the story. The app is free to use if you have your own book (library!) or a premium version gives you access to digital copies of their books as well.

- **Toy Theater** is a great, free website chock full of content-based games (math, reading, art, and music). There isn't any login, which is great for getting little learners playing and practicing quickly, but that also means you can't see student performance data captured on the back end. These would make for great brain breaks, bell ringers, or activities to fill a little bit of left over time.

- **Kiddle** is a search engine designed for little learners; it is a safe search and picture based.

RESOURCES

Items in **bold** in the text are listed here in the Resources. Direct access to all the following resources is available at https://hybridteacherresource.com and on this book's page on www.wiley.com.

Emma Chitters' Twitter—https://twitter.com/EChitters89

Seesaw—https://web.seesaw.me

Emma Chitters' Blog—https://emmachitters.wixsite.com/website/post/living-and-working-along-side-covid-19-in-luxembourg

Lisa Ann TikTok—https://www.tiktok.com/@terrificteaching/video/6874979448861527301?lang=en

Novel Effect—https://noveleffect.com

Toy Theater—https://toytheater.com

Kiddle—https://www.kiddle.co

Chapter 12
Subject-Specific Strategies

I was lucky that I met the right mentors and teachers at the right moment.
—James Levine

As I mentioned in the introduction (you read that, right?) all the advice in this book comes from my very specific lens as a middle school English teacher, which is why I also wanted to reach out to educators in different content areas and fields to get their input on what has worked best for them in hybrid and remote learning.

ENGLISH

Although I've already delved into many of my favorite tools and processes, here are a few more that are specific to an English/language arts classroom:

- **Hoopla** and **OverDrive**—Access to online ebooks and audiobook with a library card
- **Audible Stories**—Free audiobooks (COVID response)
- **Actively Learn**—Interactive, annotated texts and videos
- **Newsela**—News stories and activities adapted to different reading levels
- **Parlay**—Synchronous and asynchronous discussion platform
- **Progressive Stories via Google Docs**—A fun, remote, writing activity
- **eReading Games**—Highly addictive grammar and language review games
- **Get Epic**—Digital reading resource for K-5
- **Edji.it**—Collaborative online annotation tool
- **Story Seed Podcast**—Stories written in collaboration between students and professional authors

TAG

I would be remiss if I leave my own project, **Tag**, out of this resource list. Tag was born out of the need to help secondary students continue to learn words they are spelling incorrectly and not become too reliant on spell-check.

It is a Google Chrome extension that will capture the words students are spell-checking in their Google Docs and Slides and add them to a list that can be downloaded onto a Google Sheet.

I am currently in the process of developing **games** and assessments that can be used in conjunction with the personalized spelling lists.

Tag is very much in its early stages, and it is not a perfect product yet; but if this sounds like something valuable to you or your students, feel free to download it, test it, and give feedback at tagwords.org.

MATH

Lindsey Mater teaches 7th- and 8th-grade math at PGA and shares these thoughts:

At the middle school level, I use **Edpuzzle** for watching videos and comprehension questions, **Kami** for annotating PDFs, and **Pear Deck** to increase engagement when teaching live synchronous online classes.

Desmos is an AMAZING resource where you can assign activities and watch real-time progress during synchronous teaching. This is one of my top recommendations; it has graphic calculator activities, card sorts, and several other interactive activities, all of which are very engaging. They are low stakes for students, yet always on point with learning objectives.

Also **GeoGebra** has many useful tools and activities for many of the hands-on geometry construction standards, and **EquatIO**, which helps add mathematical symbols into text spaces.

DeltaMath is the go-to for many online instructional components for many high school math teachers (in addition to Khan).

The challenge for teachers new to online math teaching is how to not stay stuck in just teaching procedural math and fluency (**Khan** is good for this). You want to be creative to make sure conceptual understanding is also happening and real-world/application type problems as well. This is where small-group work online can often come in handy as well as synchronous class time.

Additional math resources:

- **Mathigon Polypads**—Virtual math manipulatives
- **Print Graph Paper**—Different styles of graph paper that can be printed or downloaded to be used as a background image for digital math practice
- **99 Math**—Review-style math game (Similar to Quizizz or Kahoot)
- **Math Learning Center**—Free math apps

SCIENCE

Tory Wilson teaches 6th- through 8th-grade science at PGA middle school, environmental science at PGA high school, and supports elementary science labs at PGA as well:

Tools

For EdTech tools, I use **Discovery Education** for most of my science content. I would love to explore different resources next year (such as **Newsela** and **Actively Learn**). For virtual labs, I frequently use **Gizmos** and **Phet Simulations**. I also use **Pear Deck**, **Kami**, **PlayPosit**, **TedEd**, **Amoeba Sisters videos**, and **Edpuzzle**.

Interactive Notebook

Next year I am planning to use **Seesaw** as an interactive journal. I envision assigning interactive activities in Seesaw for practice and to check for understanding. Students can respond in several different ways, offering them choices such as text, draw, video, voice, or picture, or any combinations of those.

For example, I can ask students to demonstrate their understanding of the process of photosynthesis using words and pictures.

I also want this to be a place where students can record notes as they read content in Discovery Ed or other resources, such as recording main ideas and vocabulary words (replacing a paper notebook). I really like that Seesaw keeps a log so students can easily go back and review their work and reference their previous activities and notes. With the pro account, I can leave them comments directly on their notes and activities. Last year, students used traditional paper notebooks in my class. However, this was not a useful study tool or resource to most students. Frequently, notebooks would get left at school or at home and were not available to the student when they needed it. In our hybrid environment, I want a tool that can serve students both remotely at home and in-person at school. Seesaw appears to offer a solution to this dilemma. As I was researching different tools for a digital notebook, I explored the true purpose of a notebook. I realized that a digital notebook didn't have to look exactly like a traditional paper notebook. As a digital tool that offers students choices and incorporates teacher feedback, Seesaw is a valuable EdTech tool that I will use in my hybrid classroom.

Science Labs

There are also special considerations you need to make when doing labs in the hybrid model.

I didn't do very many labs this past spring with COVID, but that is not sustainable moving forward. Labs are the best part of science and keep kids engaged. **Gizmos** and **Phet Simulations** are helpful to replace labs in a virtual environment but also aren't quite as much fun.

100% remote learning also poses more issues for labs. If we are remote, I will have to adjust labs and use more virtual simulations. I will also use **Group Activity over Google Meet** to have students work in small groups and on collaborative documents from home.

Access to tools and resources at home will be the most difficult part, but if I can overcome that, students can always record videos of lab activities they complete at home and submit those for credit online. **Seesaw** and **Flipgrid** make it easy for students to record experiments at home.

When we go back to a hybrid model, I would love to have students learn the concepts at home on remote days and then save in-person days for hands-on learning and labs, more like a flipped classroom environment. However, social distancing protocol will make in-person labs extremely challenging. We would need more supplies and it will be difficult to collaborate in groups. Tools such as **Kami** and **Google Docs**, where students can work on the same lab document while following social distancing protocols will be helpful.

Hannah McGrath, a high school science teacher, has been working at PGA since in 2009. Here are her top tips for hybrid science instruction:

I think the most helpful tip I can provide is free resources that do a great job of helping students visualize and understand difficult topics.

Favorite YouTube channels:

- **The Amoeba Sisters**: Short videos with simple explanations and fun animations. Good for introducing a topic.
- **Bozeman Science**: More detailed explanations of science concepts. Great for expanding on a topic.
- **Crash Course**: Another source of more detailed explanations, with more humor. The narrative is pretty fast though, so encourage students to turn on the captions.
- **SciShow**: An excellent resource from the same makers of Crash Course that explores random topics. Great for real-life connections and for students to explore science concepts they are interested in.

Favorite online resources for students to use:

- **The Concord Consortium**: Detailed lessons on science, technology, education, and mathematics (STEM) topics that usually feature an interactive piece for the student to complete.
- Their **Geniventure** interactive is an excellent game-based approach to explaining the role that genetics plays on the phenotype of an organism.
- **PhET**: A plethora of science simulations to use across classes. If you create a free teacher account, you gain access to lesson plans and (sometimes) answer keys.
- **Learn.Genetics**: (teacher companion site is https://teach.genetics.utah.edu/) This resource provides a ton of free videos, articles, and free resources that explain the role of genetics in simple language. They have an excellent interactive that looks at the genetics of pigeon breeding.

Emily Pontius is a high school physics and robotics teacher in New Jersey:

I have several suggestions for resources for high school (perhaps some middle school) science teachers:

- **Pivot Interactives**—Is browser based, with editable labs that include real videos (a great break from the simulations, which sometimes students don't believe/relate to), and measurement tools. It supports model-building. Large comprehensive listing of labs for physics, and building on including more chemistry, biology, and earth science.

Teachers can also create their own labs (and there is a library of these as well). They will give a teacher a 30-day trial to check it out. It is fairly low cost, at $5/student/academic year, and not student specific.

- **VEXcode VR**—Provides a virtual robot for teaching students to code either using blocks or Python that is browser based. VEX provides editable docs that are challenges/activities. They were a lifesaver last spring for my engineering physics class! Can be suitable for approximately 2nd grade through high school. Free (at the time of writing at least).

- **Tinkercad by Autodesk**—Browser-based platform for 3D-design, electric circuits (including Arduinos), and codeblocks. It comes with class management tools, which may be linked to Google Classroom. Free.

SOCIAL STUDIES

- **Smithsonian Learning Lab**—A wealth of resources that you can bundle together and share with your students to explore digitally.

- **Google Arts and Culture**—Take virtual field trips to historic sites, museums, explore artwork, and even play games.

- **Powtoon** or **Explee**—Similar to the video editing programs mentioned in Chapter 4, Apply, Create, Explore, both of these programs have free versions that allow students to create short videos. The benefits of Powtoon or Explee for a social studies class is their explanatory nature, great for summarizing or explaining historical events.

- **iCivics**—Founded by US Supreme Court Justice Sandra Day O'Connor, iCivics is a free, game-based website where students play in order to learn about American civics.

- **Wonderopolis**—Odd and interesting "wonders" and accompanying articles and videos help stoke students' curiosity on local and global phenomena. Ever wonder what Geocatching is? Wonderopolis has your answer.

- **Timeline**—A free website that takes students through a step-by-step guide to creating a beautiful, interactive timeline using a Google Sheet template.

- **History Pin**—Is a crowdsourced, collaborative website where users can explore historical topics and see where events occurred on a local level by clicking into pins on a map. Then, users can upload their own information, photos, and pins by creating a new "collection." It would be a great site to use when learning about local history.

WORLD LANGUAGES

- **Seesaw**—Use the quick and easy access to video and audio recording to hear your students practicing vocabulary or conversations.

- **Quizlet**—Flash card–based review website. Teachers can create vocabulary-based flash card decks to share with students, or students can create their own. Quizlet offers programs that help students learn and practice words including quizzes and games.

- **Duolingo**—Popular, free language acquisition app. Use as a supplement to your curriculum or as an option for emergency sub plans.

- **Memrise**—Similar to Duolingo, Memrise is a language acquisition program enhanced by short, high-quality videos of native language speakers demonstrating the pronunciation and context of a word or phrase. Memrise has free and premium courses.

- **Forvo**—Is a pronunciation website. Whereas many people go to Google Translate to hear the correct pronunciation of words and often get a poor computerized version, Forvo asks users and native language speakers to record the pronunciations themselves. Students can use the website to seek out pronunciations, or better yet, you can practice pronunciation then submit your own recordings. I'm not going to lie, it is strangely addicting.

- **Google Translate**—As I'm sure all language teachers are aware, Google Translate is a tool students need no help in discovering.

Instead of fighting against Google Translate, incorporate it into some of your activities. Ask students to write a sentence in their native language, translate it into the foreign language, then spend the lesson practice checking the accuracy of the translation and editing it for improvement.

You could also create an assignment where you ask students to give you the Google Translation of a phrase, then ask them to think of another way they could express the same idea.

VISUAL ART

Cole Zawadski is a former high school and current elementary art teacher.

At our school, all of our remote synchronous learning happens on Microsoft Teams. I join classroom meetings when it is our special time and "take over" for a short amount of time. I typically begin class with a 5–10 minute mini lesson, which might look like a screen-share (which I really appreciate the convenience of) and discussion of an artwork, a short video/tutorial, or an inquiry question to prompt some deeper level thinking before artmaking.

Then, I like to give the majority of the class time to work on personal artworks, which is typically accompanied by an instrumental chillhop backdrop DJed by Mr. Z and a plethora of YouTube mixes. With a few minutes left, I have my students clean up their workspace and "home" studio to prepare for a class share time.

My art teaching model is inspired by the Teaching for Artistic Behavior approach to art education. Many art teachers might also know it as a "choice-based" approach. The premise being that an art teacher's job is not to manage the what and how of the art students' creation but more so facilitating the exploration, curiosity, and choice in their own artistic pursuits. The focus is less on creating a cute little artwork to take home and hang on the fridge, and more on developing the transferrable and relatable skills an artist utilizes on the daily in their studio practice. Many art educators, including myself, refer to these as the Studio Habits of Mind (SHoM), a set of eight distinct "habits" that studio artists participate in according to Harvard's Project Zero framework.

This year I have been designing my curriculum around grade level themes, like 1st grade's theme, artists tell stories through their art. Occasionally I have a more specific prompt, but more often than not, I share new ideas, questions, and ways to use materials that inform their artmaking. The choice as to what to make art with and about is in their hands, hearts, and heads (that is what I use to organize SHoM skills in a simpler fashion).

Students use what they have available to them at home to create art. For the majority of what we've been doing synchronously, that is tangible materials (pencil, paper, scissors, glue, crayons, markers, colored pencil, playdough, found object, recycled materials, slime). I think the opportunity to work in the company of each other with tangible materials maintains some semblance of normalcy, even if it is in another location in front of a camera. Most of the digital tools they use asynchronously on Seesaw or from my Bitmoji classroom.

When it is time to share, the screen-sharing feature is simple but effective in assisting the focus of the class to the topic/artwork at hand. I feel like in a typical classroom environment, I am battling projection quality and consistency issues and having to consider the physical arrangement of the classroom and students to ensure an effective presentation on screen. With a screen share, it is right there in front of them and I can still see them and respond to their questions, comments, and body language with the help of a dual screen.

I love dual screens. I tried a few times managing a screen full of students and the content I was trying to share and use during class on the same monitor, and it wasn't easy or very fun. When considering the two camps of duplicators or extenders, I am definitely an extender. I like having my material or "things for the teacher" on one side and "things for my students on the other." Then I don't run the risk of distracting my students with anything irrelevant to their learning in the moment. I think most teachers have gotten caught in random tangents that can suck from meaningful learning time, and minimizing the chance of something on the screen prompting one is helpful.

The other big tool I use is **Seesaw**. It is essentially a digital portfolio/asynchronous learning platform. I love it and have used it as a way for students to showcase their learning and me to respond and offer feedback in ways that wouldn't have been possible in a synchronous capacity, mostly due to time.

Additional visual art resources:

- **Google Drawing**—Web-based design tool; users can free draw or use lines and shapes to create digital art.

- **Infinite Painter**—Is a Chromebook app that allows touch screen users a realistic painting experience with options for customized brush strokes and colors.

- **Google Arts and Culture**—Is difficult to categorize as there are so many different experiences from creating your own artwork by coloring in famous paintings to exploring actual museum exhibits in VR to turning your own face into a Van Gogh style painting.

- **Smart History**—An art history teaching resource.

- **Autodesk Sketchbook**—Digital sketching app.

DRAMA

Gavin Foster is an elementary music, drama, and dance teacher based in Ontario, Canada, as well as a Global Google for Educator Group leader:

- **QWappy Improv**—A great app for drama or theater teachers, preloaded with hundreds of improv games that can be filtered by categories such as individual, group, guessing, bizarre, scene suggestions, and more (see Figure 12.1).

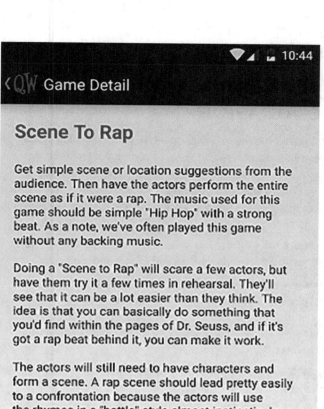

Figure 12.1: Qwappy Improve app.

- **Dramarts**—A free app for drama teachers or directors to organize a cast. Features include scheduling, communication, and digital script editing.

- **Script Rehearser**—Is a free app that allows users to upload a script and practice their lines with a computerized voice reading the other lines.

PHYSICAL EDUCATION

Physical education is a difficult class to translate into remote learning, as so much of the activities are collaborative and team based. However, as adults we are often engaging in physical activity independently and using digital resources (apps and YouTube videos) to do so, so teaching students how to stay active independently at home is an important life skill that, it is hoped, they will carry with them into adulthood.

- **GoNoodle**—Is chock full of great movement videos, including easy and more difficult choreographed dance routines, yoga, and exercise.
- **Just Dance Now**—A popular dance-based video game. Students will need individual devices (phones or tablets) with the app downloaded to track their movements and score points in the dance. If students don't have access to individual devices, you can have students follow along on the **YouTube channel**.
- **Nike Training Club**—Another app that requires students to have access to individual devices, Nike Training Club offers short (and longer) strength, cardio, and mobility exercises, most of which don't require equipment.
- **Sworkit**—A similar program to Nike Training Club, Sworkit has exercises designed and modeled by kids and also has an educators' initiative where teachers can sign up to use the program for free and in doing so customize or create workouts for their students.

MUSIC

Theresa Hoover teaches middle school band, is a Google Certified Innovator, and the author of "Pass the Baton."

Her approach to hybrid and remote music instruction is to ensure that students are driving the learning and creating. She said, "Students are in a band because they want to make music with their friends."

One way she facilitates this is by using collaborative Google Slides and breakout rooms. Each group of students will have a shared Google Slide deck that they can all work on together, and then will be put into a breakout room where they will be asked to research a piece of music.

Other times she will ask students to collaborate on music creation in their breakout rooms, typically with a tool called **Noteflight**, an online music notation tool where students can compose their own songs and collaborate.

When students aren't collaborating, they might be using **Google Arts and Culture** to explore a virtual museum exhibit (such as the **American Jazz Museum** in Kansas City) or even watch a performance (such as performances at the Kennedy Center and even **Carnegie Hall**) This is typically an independent exploration coupled with a summary of what they learned (or a **PMI** [Plusses, Minuses and Interesting things] chart), great for asynchronous lessons.

For playing and performing music, Hoover acknowledged the difficulty of practicing as a group whenever a video conferencing platform is involved (because of the lag times in video and audio transmission). However, she also recognized a benefit to her school's COVID response, in that there was no concert or musical showcase to prepare for, which allowed her to focus on the students as individual musicians and allowed her students to focus more on creation.

Some of her favorite tools for student music creation and assessment include:

- **Flipgrid**—Students record short music performances that Hoover can watch privately and provide encouragement and feedback on (in a moderated setting). Or she'll ask students to record videos for their fellow classmates to watch and leave feedback on, teaching them how to listen and articulate. She also recognizes the opportunity for student musicians to use Flipgrid to collaborate and improvise, by responding to video clips of musical riffs with their own additions (high school jazz, for example).

- **Chrome Music Lab**—Has plenty of fun tools for students to play with and explore, but Hoover uses the "song maker" most frequently, as teachers can create a template or a melody for students to work off of.

- **Smart Music**—Provides access to music online and teachers can listen to student's music and give them feedback on which notes they are playing correctly/incorrectly.

- **Garage Band**—A fully equipped music creation studio for students and teachers with access to Apple devices (including iPads and Macs).

Lesson Plan

Subject: Band

Topic: Note identification

For May 4 (Sometimes known as Star Wars Day), put the first part of the Star Wars melody in **song maker** on Chrome Music Lab and instruct students to finish the melody.

Additional music resources:

- **Sound Trap**—Browser-based, collaborative music creation studio.
- **Flat**—Browser-based, collaborative music composition tool.

RESOURCES

Items in **bold** in the text are listed here in the Resources. Direct access to all the following resources is available at https://hybridteacherresource.com and on this book's page on www.wiley.com.

Hoopla—https://www.hoopladigital.com

OverDrive—https://www.overdrive.com

Actively Learn—https://www.activelylearn.com

Audible Stories—https://stories.audible.com

Newsela—https://newsela.com

Parlay—https://parlayideas.com

Progressive Stories via Google Docs—https://www.edtechemma.com/single-post/2020/05/14/Progressive-Stories-via-Google-Docs

eReading Games—https://ereadinggames.com

Get Epic—https://www.getepic.com

Edji—https://edji.it/#/home

Story Seed Podcast—https://www.storyseedspodcast.com

Tag—https://www.tagwords.org

Practice Through Play—Tag—https://www.tagwords.org/play

Lindsey Mater's Twitter—https://twitter.com/MaterTwo

Edpuzzle—https://edpuzzle.com/content

Kami—https://www.kamiapp.com

Pear Deck—https://www.peardeck.com/googleslides

Desmos—https://www.desmos.com

GeoGebra—https://www.geogebra.org/?lang=en

EquatIO—https://chrome.google.com/webstore/detail/equatio-math-made-digital/hjngolefdpdnooamgdldlkjgmdcmcjnc?hl=en-US

DeltaMath—https://deltamath.com

Khan—https://www.khanacademy.org

Mathigon—https://mathigon.org/polypad

Print Graph Paper—https://print-graph-paper.com

99 Math—https://99math.com

Math Learning Center—https://www.mathlearningcenter.org/apps

Tory Wilson Twitter—https://twitter.com/torycwilson

Discovery Education—https://www.discoveryeducation.com

Actively Learn—https://www.activelylearn.com

Gizmos—https://www.explorelearning.com

PhET Simulations—https://phet.colorado.edu

PlayPosit—https://go.playposit.com

TedEd—https://ed.ted.com

Amoeba Sisters Videos—https://www.youtube.com/user/AmoebaSisters

Group Activity over Google Meet—https://www.edtechemma.com/single-post/2020/03/26/Group-Activity-over-Google-Meet

Seesaw—https://web.seesaw.me

FlipGrid—https://info.flipgrid.com

Bozeman Science—https://www.youtube.com/channel/UCEik-U3T6u6JA0XiHLbNbOw

Crash Course—https://www.youtube.com/user/crashcourse

SciShow—https://www.youtube.com/user/scishow

The Concord Consortium—https://learn.concord.org

GeniVenture—https://learn.concord.org/geniventure

Learn.Genetics—https://learn.genetics.utah.edu

Pigeon Breeding—https://learn.genetics.utah.edu/content/pigeons/

Pivot Interactives—https://www.pivotinteractives.com

VEXCode VR—https://www.vexrobotics.com/vexcode-vr

Tinkercad by Autodesk—https://www.tinkercad.com/teach

Smithsonian Learning Lab—https://learninglab.si.edu

Google Arts and Culture—https://artsandculture.google.com

PowToon—https://www.powtoon.com/premium/

ExPlee—https://explee.com

iCivics—https://www.icivics.org/our-story

Wonderopolis—https://wonderopolis.org/wonders

Timeline—https://timeline.knightlab.com

History Pin—https://www.historypin.org/en/

Quizlet—https://quizlet.com/latest

Duolingo—https://www.duolingo.com

Memrise—https://app.memrise.com/home/

Forvo—https://forvo.com/languages/es/

Google Translate—https://translate.google.com

Google Drawing—https://docs.google.com/drawings

Infinite Painter—https://chromebookapphub.withgoogle.com/apps/infinite-painter

Smart History—https://smarthistory.org

Autodesk Sketchbook—https://www.commonsense.org/education/app/autodesk-sketchbook

QWappy Improv—https://appgrooves.com/android/com.clumsygiant.ultimateimprov/qwappy-improv/clumsy-giant-inc

Dramarts—https://www.dramarts.com/landing

Script Rehearser—https://apps.apple.com/us/app/script-rehearser/id1441908800

GoNoodle—https://app.gonoodle.com

Just Dance Now—https://justdancenow.com

Just Dance YouTube Channel—https://www.youtube.com/channel/UC0Vlh-de7N5uGDIFXXWWEbFQ

Nike Training Club—https://www.nike.com/ntc-app

Sworkit—https://sworkit.com/youth-initiative

Noteflight—https://www.noteflight.com

The American Jazz Museum—https://artsandculture.google.com/partner/american-jazz-museum

Carnegie Hall Performances—https://performingarts.withgoogle.com/en_us/performances/carnegie-hall

PMI Chart—https://www.worksheetworks.com/miscellanea/graphic-organizers/pmi.html

Chrome Music Lab—https://musiclab.chromeexperiments.com

Smart Music—https://www.smartmusic.com

GarageBand—https://www.apple.com/mac/garageband/

Music Lab Song Maker—https://musiclab.chromeexperiments.com/Song-Maker/

SoundTrap—https://www.soundtrap.com

Flat—https://flat.io

Chapter 13
Nonteaching Staff

You are only as good as your team.

—Dominique Wilkins

Although this book is written for teachers, I am fully aware of the importance of our schools' nonteaching staff who aid in student care and learning, without whom we couldn't do our jobs successfully.

The following tips and tools might be helpful to nonteaching staff in a hybrid or emergency remote scenario.

PARAS

When teachers are lucky enough to have paraprofessionals in the classroom, those paras often support students with their executive functioning skills (helping students focus, initiate tasks, organize) or work with small groups or one on one with students for practice and assessment.

In a virtual classroom, paras can still support in numerous ways. First, they can play the role of "moderator," helping to mute students who haven't done so themselves, and answer student questions or redirect off-topic comments in the chat box.

Paras can help monitor participation data during class, noting how many times any one student contributed a response by chatting in the chat box or unmuting their microphones. During breakout rooms, paras can be placed with a small group of students to lead a targeted intervention session or even be placed in a breakout room one on one with the students they support.

Paras might also help by assessing or marking digital work, if you are able to add them as a "co-teacher" to your Google Classroom or other learning management system.

LIBRARIANS

First and foremost librarians can help students access books digitally. Many local libraries work with companies like **OverDrive** and **Hoopla** to provide digital access to books, audiobooks, and other media. Ensuring students have access to sites like these would be incredibly valuable.

Librarians can provide digital and technical support. They might consider hosting a virtual "Help Desk" where students can click a link to join a video conference and ask technical questions about the platforms they are using for their classes for assignments.

STUDENT AIDES

There are plenty of roles student aides can play in a virtual environment including:

- Moderator—making sure the students are on topic in the chat and alerting the teacher when there is a question.
- Classroom librarian—Updating the list of digital books available to students or making recommendations.
- Badge designer—If you are using digital badges, your student aide could design them in a tool like Google Drawings or Canva.
- Prompt creator—If you are looking for a fun community question or writing prompt, task your student aide with writing or researching it.

- Video curator—If you play music before class or enjoy showing a "Friday Fun" video, ask your student aide to make a playlist of these.
- Technical support—If your student aide is technically adept, put them in a breakout room with a student/s who is having technical difficulties during class.

RESOURCES

Items in **bold** in the text are listed here in the Resources. Direct access to all the following resources is available at https://hybridteacherresource.com and on this book's page on www.wiley.com.

OverDrive—https://www.overdrive.com

Hoopla—https://www.hoopladigital.com

Chapter 14
Adapting

If a child can't learn the way we teach, maybe we should teach the way they learn.

—Ignacio "Nacho" Estrada

As I mentioned in the introduction, this book was written from my perspective as a mainstream middle school English teacher in a hybrid school in Colorado. The chance that anyone reading this shares my exact same lens and experience is pretty slim. We all come from unique backgrounds with unique challenges and skills that inform how we show up. Not only we teachers but our students as well.

The following sections attempt to demonstrate how we might respond to some of our learners' unique needs.

SPECIAL EDUCATION

Like most teachers, I keep a list of the individualized education program (IEP) and 504 requirements for each of my students close at hand when planning lessons and assignments. Although some common accommodations translate well to a virtual environment (i.e. extended time), others (i.e. preferred seating) don't.

The most common accommodation I've seen teachers using with special education students in a remote environment is leveraging their paras and teaching assistants to meet with students one on one over video conferencing.

Putting a para or co-teacher in a breakout room with that student during independent work time is a great way to ensure they are having their needs met during remote synchronous instruction. Also, asking paras and co-teachers to use a private chat channel (in Zoom, Google Chat, or Microsoft Teams) during direct instruction to ask students comprehension questions or to answer student questions in a private channel is another great way to use their support.

During asynchronous workdays, it is helpful to schedule office hours and provide a link to a video conference call for students to join if questions arise.

When I am assisting students over a video call, I ask the student to share their screen with me so they can drive the learning. I simply use my voice to coach them when necessary. We are also frequently working on a collaborative document (like a Google Doc or Google Slide), so I can make edits or comments directly on the document that they can see in real time.

There are many other digital tools that can help you adapt and differentiate for your students:

- **Differentiate Google Classroom Assignments**

    When it comes to differentiating work for my students, the most powerful tool I've found is the ability to post work to individuals or groups of students in Google Classroom (see Figure 14.1). Notice on the right-hand side how Patty is unselected and will not be receiving this version of the assignment.

Figure 14.1: Selecting students for a Google Classroom assignment.

Often what I'll do is post one assignment for the majority of the class, then **click the "reuse post" button** and post the same work again (with scaffolds) for the students for whom I am differentiating. This allows me to edit the instructions or adapt the assignment slightly to meet their individual needs.

Doing this makes it quick and easy to ensure that students are getting the appropriate amount of work or scaffolding to help them succeed.

- Device-Specific Accessibility Tools

Regardless of the device your students use, there will be specific accessibility tools built in to help all learners with their specific needs.

For example, Chromebooks have an accessibility menu on the dashboard that will allow the user to enlarge their mouse and use dictation tools, high-contrast screens, and magnifiers. **Cat Lamin**, UK-based EdTech consultant for **Canopy**, has made a set of **Google Accessibility Flashcards** for quick access and reminders on how to differentiate with Chromebooks or the Chrome web browser.

- Speech to Text

One of my favorite accessibility tools is speech to text. There is a dictation feature built into many devices that will allow you to dictate into any place where text can be typed.

There is also a speech-to-text feature built right into Google Docs. Simply click "tools" and "voice typing" in a Google Doc, and you will see a microphone icon (Figure 14.2). Below that is a dropdown menu to select the language in which you plan to dictate.

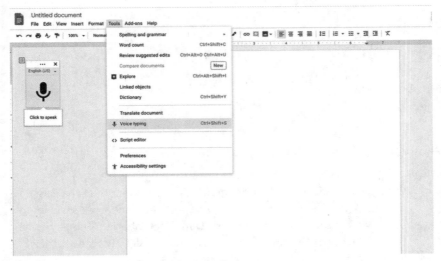

Figure 14.2: Voice typing in Google Docs.

Although the accuracy of the dictation isn't perfect (and there is a lot to be desired on the punctuation side of things) students who struggle with writing or typing can get a good start on a digital writing assignment simply through dictation.

I love to use this feature with my students who have dyslexia, are English language learners, or struggle with typing and spelling. Getting most of your ideas down on the page through voice makes a large writing assignment feel much more manageable.

- Closed Captions

Closed captions are a great option for the deaf and hard of hearing, English language learners, or distracted students.

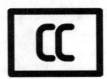

PowerPoint, Google Slides, and Google Meet all have a closed caption feature that can be turned on or off and will do its best to capture your voice as you give your lesson at the top or bottom of the screen.

- Read & Write

  Read & Write is a popular Chrome extension that does a number of things for students struggling with their literacy, including text to speech and speech to text, picture dictionaries, word prediction, annotation tools, voice notes, and page-declutter.

  Read & Write is a paid-for product.

- Declutter and Distraction Extensions

  There are also a number of free Chrome extensions, such as **Adblock Plus**, that will help eliminate ad banners and other distracting clutter from a webpage, so your easily distracted-students can remain focused on the task at hand.

  Other extensions, such as **Block Site**, can help maintain focus by temporarily blocking or limiting time spent on distracting websites (i.e. Twitter, Facebook, Instagram.)

  Finally, there are extensions, like **Forest**, that turn online productivity into a game by allowing students to "grow" digital plants based on the time they spend on-task on their computer.

  Any of these tools could help students self-regulate their time and attention.

- Visibility Tools

  As mentioned previously in Chapter 5, Keep Design in Mind, there are usually some great visibility tools built into whichever device you or your student are using, such as screen magnifiers, and high-contrast mode, but you also might consider using a color contrast checker when you are designing your lessons.

  In her book *The Perfect Blend*, Michelle Eaton recommends using a tool like **WebAIM** to ensure any students with visual impairments (including colorblindness) are able to clearly see color distinctions in your lesson.

WebAIM will allow you to do a quick check of the compatibility of the colors you are planning to use, and it will even distinguish between compatibility with different font types and sizes.

Although, as a classroom teacher, it is my job to make sure I am making accommodations for my students with IEPs and 504s, special education teachers have even more to consider in a hybrid or remote environment.

Dr. Aime Sharp is a Gifted and Talented Coordinator and Interventionist at PSD Global Academy (PGA) who holds a master's in special education and a doctorate of education in curriculum and instruction for gifted students. She shares these thoughts:

I think the biggest thing with special education remotely is being able to adhere as much as possible to the hours/minutes that are written in a student's IEP. This is actually easier with a student who has academic needs and can be tutored individually through meetings that can help and give more specific one on one attention. The important thing with this from a legal perspective is that any attempts to meet the service-hour requirements is documented by whomever is doing that work.

The other suggestion that I would make with this is that doing some type of a project-based lesson that incorporates several different subjects is a better way of engaging these students in a remote learning setting. In this special education role, I have found that instead of just supporting students in doing the general education work, that I and many of the other special education teachers have been able to be more creative in producing individualized project-based lessons that are tailored more specifically to each student's needs and interests.

The biggest struggle that I have found is supporting students with behavioral needs remotely. We accomplished this fairly well with assigning the behavioral support paras that would normally be working with the children in a classroom to meeting online with those children during those same times and supporting them with their online work as much as possible. This worked for the times when the students would normally be in a face-to-face classroom but did not help with the times that they were normally not supported and did not help as much with relationships with peers online or with their families while they were at home.

My sense of what could possibly benefit these students more is a tag-team approach where many different general education teachers, special education teachers, paraprofessionals, mental health specialists, counselors and even administrators work together to check in with the student more frequently but also work with the parents or guardians to train them in behavioral management techniques and give them as much remote support as possible. This type of cooperation might necessitate the rewriting/amending of IEPs to support students in remote learning environments.

ENGLISH LANGUAGE LEARNERS

Staying connected with students is considerably more challenging when there is a language barrier between you and your students and/or you and your students' parents.

Make an extra effort to keep these students engaged through the use of these tools.

- **Google Translate**—Not only available on its website, but can also be used in Google Docs to translate entire documents; on the Chrome browser to translate webpages; and on the app, which allows you to take a photo of handwritten text, signs, or pages in a book and translate those as well.

- **Read & Write**—As mentioned earlier in this chapter, this software helps with literacy and language acquisition using a variety of tools.

- **Microsoft Translator**—Similar to closed captions, Microsoft Translator will actually translate live speech into second language text on a PowerPoint presentation.

- **Immersive Reader**—Similar to Read & Write, Immersive Reader helps students with literacy and language acquisition. However, it is specific to Microsoft products like Word and OneNote.

Aubrey Yeh, an administrator at Boulder Valley Public School District, has worked with student refugees for over 10 years, most of whom are English language learners.

She believes that ensuring your English language learners (ELL) understand their systems and technology is of utmost importance for remote learning. Her district provides instructional videos in both English and Spanish, but for many of her refugee students who speak more obscure native languages, she finds meeting with them one on one (in person or over Google Meet) is the best way to navigate new digital spaces. Using **custom cursors** could help students follow along, especially when language is a barrier.

Aubrey emphasizes that it is equally important to ensure that the parents of ELL understand both the technology and the expectations for how their students should be engaging in their work. She reminds us that many parents of ELL, particularly refugees, come from cultures where the expectation and system of education is entirely different from our own. We need to be explicit and clear about what the student should be doing at home, for how long, and how it will be assessed.

Yeh told me a story of a conference she had with a refugee student and parent in which the teacher explained that the student had a "C" in the class and why. It wasn't until after the conference had ended that the parent asked Aubrey what a "C" was.

We often take basic knowledge of our own country's education and technology for granted and need to remember that not all students and parents have the same foundational knowledge.

For communicating with parents, Yeh has found that text messaging is often the most accessible method. (I use **Google Voice**, a free app that will provide you with a different phone number, when conferencing or texting parents from home, to protect my personal phone number.) If her ELL families are having difficulty with their devices and can't meet online, she will often ask them to take images of what they are seeing on their screens and text them to her. Then she will respond by sending her own image, using pointers and other visuals, to indicate where the student or parent needs to go.

Once her students and parents are comfortable with the technology and understand the academic expectations, Yeh recommends delivering content with simplicity and consistency. Although choice-boards are great for many students, she recommends differentiating for ELL by limiting the amount of sites they need to visit, and staying consistent in the programs you are asking them to use. Then, you could help your students bookmark those sites so they are easy to access.

ACCESS TO TECHNOLOGY

At the onset of COVID-19 school closures, one of the common strategies adopted by schools and districts was to send paper packets home with students to complete and then return to the school building for teachers to grade.

Ultimately, I don't object to this model. It ensures that all students have access to their materials and there is a system in place for the collection and dispensation of such.

But I think we can do better.

Paper packets do not allow for immediate feedback. Paper packets do not allow for connection and communication with peers. Paper packets do not translate into practical and applicable tech skills.

All districts should be working as hard as they possibly can at the beginning of each school year (not just in a pandemic) to ensure that all students have access to Wi-Fi and a digital learning device at home.

The support for this ultimately needs to come from the state and federal government to provide the funding.

While we work toward that, here are a few ideas to get you started with what you have available to you:

- Neverware

  Neverware in an amazing software that can take most used/outdated devices, wipe them clean of their operating system, and give them new life as a Chromebook by installing Chrome OS.

  I have personally done this with an old Mac laptop that I used for far too long, and it significantly increased the speed and usability of that old device.

  If your school has outdated devices that are unusable because of their speed, Neverware could be a viable alternative to purchasing new devices. Your school or district could also consider asking for donations or purchasing old devices to Neverware.

Neverware is free to use. However, if you'd like a "management license" for the device (which enables you to control the device through the Google Admin Console) there is a fee per device.

- Personal Hotspots

    Many districts, including my own, worked hard in the initial shutdown to provide personal hotspots to families who didn't have reliable internet access.

    However, hotspots can be expensive, costing on average $100–150/hotspot, plus an additional monthly service fee of around $15–20/month.

- Partnering with Local Businesses and Internet Service Providers (ISP)

    Cody Holt, Coordinator of Instructional Design and C4L Program Manager at Royse City Independent School District, had an innovative idea to partner with local businesses to provide Wi-Fi to students in their surrounding areas:

    > We supported students without Wi-Fi in a few different ways. Several years ago we asked local businesses if they would be willing to provide free Wi-Fi access for students while in their business. Those that agreed (which was most) were published to a list and we talked about "tagging" their storefront with a sticker as well, but the sticker never happened (wasn't needed). That obviously didn't help much during the COVID shutdown so we did a couple more things.

First, we compiled a list of all the ISPs with coverage in our district and what their current deals were for customers (most were offering deals because of COVID). We published that list for students and parents to see.

Second, we partnered with one ISP to put external wireless hotspots in six areas around our community. These "Drive Up Hotspots" allowed students to work while sitting at those locations. We are extending this program by adding six more locations in partnership with one of our hardware vendors.

- Offline Documents

  Although having reliable internet access is essential to fully engaging students in remote learning, it is worth noting that Google files can be **made available to be worked on offline**. The document will still be able to be accessed through Google Drive or Classroom initially, but will temporarily be saved to your device until you have internet connection again, at which point the file will automatically save to the cloud.

DATA AND PRIVACY

In the US education system we have two primary laws protecting students' data and privacy: The Family Educational Rights and Privacy Act (FERPA) and Children's Online Privacy Protection Rule (COPPA).

FERPA gives families the right to access their student's education records and also protects the mishandling of student information that could be considered harmful if released.

COPPA, according to The Education Framework, "prohibits unfair and/or deceptive practices in connection with the collection, use, and disclosure of personal information online from children under the age of 13." COPPA exists to regulate companies, but often schools act in place of parents to give students consent to use a website or online program. So it's important to know if that program is collecting student data, and if so, what said data are being used for.

If you do not live in the United States, check which data and privacy laws your country has adopted for education.

There is a lot to consider when vetting a web-based educational tool, and typically districts or schools have a process for vetting and approving apps and programs. When in doubt, contact your IT department for further guidance!

RESOURCES

Items in **bold** in the text are listed here in the Resources. Direct access to all the following resources is available at https://hybridteacherresource.com and on this book's page on www.wiley.com.

Differentiate Google Classroom Assignments—https://shakeuplearning.com/blog/how-to-differentiate-assignments-in-google-classroom/

Reuse a post—https://support.google.com/edu/classroom/answer/6272593?co=GENIE.Platform%3DAndroid&hl=en

Cat Lamin's Twitter—https://twitter.com/CatLamin?ref_src=twsrc%5Egoogle%7Ctwcamp%5Eserp%7Ctwgr%5Eauthor

Canopy—https://www.canopy.education

Google Accessibility Flashcards—https://drive.google.com/file/d/1RVHTyK5nwauh1UXShOVWovj9CpQOeK19/view?usp=sharing

Read & Write—https://chrome.google.com/webstore/detail/readwrite-for-google-chro/inoeonmfapjbbkmdafoankkfajkcphgd?hl=en-US

AdBlock Plus—https://chrome.google.com/webstore/detail/block-site-website-blocke/eiimnmioipafcokbfikbljfdeojpcgbh?hl=en-US

BlockSite—https://chrome.google.com/webstore/detail/block-site-website-blocke/eiimnmioipafcokbfikbljfdeojpcgbh?hl=en-US

Forest—https://chrome.google.com/webstore/detail/forest-stay-focused-be-pr/kjacjjdnoddnpbbcjilcajfhhbdhkpgk?hl=en-US

"The Perfect Blend"—https://www.thriftbooks.com/w/the-perfect-blend-a-practical-guide-to-designing-student-centered-learning-experiences_michele-eaton/25861511/item/38568064/

WebAIM—https://webaim.org/resources/contrastchecker/

Google Translate—https://translate.google.com

Microsoft Translator—https://www.microsoft.com/en-us/translator/

Immersive Reader—https://www.onenote.com/learningtools

Aubrey Yeh's Twitter—https://twitter.com/Ms_A_Yeh?ref_src=twsrc%5Egoogle%7Ctwcamp%5Eserp%7Ctwgr%5Eauthor

Custom Cursors—https://chrome.google.com/webstore/detail/custom-cursor-for-chrome/ogdlpmhglpejoiomcodnpjnfgcpmgale/related

Google Voice—https://voice.google.com/u/0/calls

Neverware—https://www.neverware.com/#intro

Work on Google Docs, Sheets, and Slides offline—https://support.google.com/docs/answer/6388102?co=GENIE.Platform%3DDesktop&hl=en

Chapter 15
Parent/Guardian Communication

Education is a shared commitment between dedicated teachers, motivated students and enthusiastic parents with high expectations.

—*Bob Beauprez*

One of the potential benefits to teaching in a hybrid model is fostering a closer relationship with parents and guardians, who are called learning coaches at PSD Global Academy (PGA). When students are working at home or remotely, learning coaches need to play a greater role as co-teachers or tutors for their students.

But there is a big difference in the amount of involvement required from learning coaches depending on the age or ability of the student. The learning coaches of elementary students tend to be the most involved and act as "co-teachers," whereas learning coaches of middle and high school students tend to play a more supportive role as "tutor" or "manager."

Regardless, it is important to ensure that learning coaches feel like they have the information, skills, and resources to assist their students at home.

PGA middle school has several methods for parent communication:

- Pioneer 100

  At PGA middle school, we start the year with a technology bootcamp and introduction to the school that we call "Pioneer 100." It is entirely online and asynchronous, and learning coaches are expected to complete portions of it with their students, so we can ensure they are trained in the fundamentals of the learning management system and other important tools, practices, and protocols.

  See Chapter 16, Technology Bootcamp, for more on this.

- Ongoing Workshops and Learning Symposiums

  We also hold ongoing learning coach workshops throughout the school year, ranging from technical (i.e. Navigating Google Classroom) to pedagogical topics such as "Asking Questions to Improve Understanding," "Building Executive Functioning Skills," and "Understanding the Teenage Brain." Typically, these are delivered both in person after on-campus school days and online via Google Meet so parents have the opportunity to attend if getting to the school building is difficult. Conducting these over Google Meet also allows us the opportunity to record our sessions so that we can post or send them to parents to watch at a later day or time.

- Learning Coach Checks

  Stacy Denham, a 6th-grade English teacher, interventionist, and middle school team lead at PGA, came up with the idea to include "Learning Coach Checks" in our Google Classroom instructions.

  In a secondary environment, some of our learning coaches were struggling to hold their students accountable for their remote work without going through the entire assignment to understand the expectations. A "Learning Coach Check" (Figure 15.1) is a short, specific observation the learning coach can make to determine whether the student has completed the work, without needing to assess the accuracy or quality (which the teacher will do).

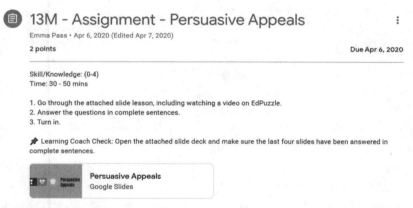

Figure 15.1: Learning coach checks in Google Classroom assignments.

These typically look like this: "Open the attached Google Slides and make sure a full paragraph has been written on slide #5" or "Open the Google Form and ensure it has been submitted."

We aren't asking parents to assess the work or even give feedback, that is the teacher's job and we will do that part once we have time to grade it, but having the support of learning coaches in making sure the work got turned in is invaluable.

- Learning Coach PDF

   We also like to provide our learning coaches a simple flyer at the start of each year to remind them of basic practices to help establish healthy work habits and routines (executive functioning skills) from home. (See Figure 15.2.)

---

2. Make Habits and Routines

An at-home school day is still a school day. Depending on your school, you might have some flexibility in the hours, but students should still be engaging in meaningful learning for 6-8 hours.

Create a schedule of what subjects you'll work on and when. Block out time for lunch, and time to move or play outside.

Making a schedule means you will be more likely to stick to it.

Also, try to stick to regular routines. Get up, eat breakfast, get dressed. My husband, who works from home, sometimes even "commutes" by going on a walk outside to clear his head and get in the right mindset before he comes back home and goes straight to his office to work.

Figure 15.2: Learning coach PDF.

- Parent–Teacher Conferences

   Although parent–teachers conferences have been a long-lasting school tradition, consider the following innovations:

   Hybrid Conference Options—For a lot of parents, making it to the school building after work for parent–teacher conferences can be challenging, if not impossible; as teachers, you know the parents you need to see most are often the ones who don't end up making it at all. Offering some in-person and some virtual conferences ensures that more parents will be able to access conference time in the mode that suits them best.

Listening Conferences—For fall semester conferences, rather than have the teacher tell the parent about their student (with the little information they have so far), consider flipping the script and asking the parent to talk to you about their student. Provide a list of questions for the parent to work from (i.e. what are your goals for your student this year? Is there anything we need to know about your student as a learner? etc.), and simply listen. When we have done this, we have gained so much valuable insight into our students that we might not have gotten otherwise.

Sign-Up Genius—For scheduling parent–teacher conferences, there are plenty of potential platforms, and although Sign-Up Genius may initially appear a little outdated, it is the simplest free tool that I've found to help organize which parents will be conferencing during each time slot.

- Weekly Communication

Learning coaches also receive ongoing communication from PGA teachers in a variety of ways.

Friday Focus is a weekly newsletter that we send to all learning coaches. It includes a "tip of the week," announcements and reminders, as well as a summary and photo from each teacher about what students worked on in that content area.

Google Classroom Guardian Summaries are offered to all learning coaches. The summaries allow them to see a daily or weekly recap of all the assignments and announcements for each content area/Google Classroom their student is enrolled in.

Although it is helpful to stay consistent in the delivery of all class/school communication (via email + Friday Focus), I've found that when it comes to communicating with individual parents about their student's performance, it is helpful to ask which method of communication they prefer.

Some parents are actively checking email, whereas others will be much more responsive via phone or text. Surveying parents at the start of the year, and saving that information on a spreadsheet is a helpful way to keep track.

I use **Google Voice**, a free app that will provide you with a different phone number, when conferencing or texting parents from home, to protect my personal phone number.

RESOURCES

Items in **bold** in the text are listed here in the Resources. Direct access to all the following resources is available at https://hybridteacherresource.com and on this book's page on www.wiley.com.

Sign-Up Genius—https://www.signupgenius.com

Google Classroom Guardian Summaries—https://support.google.com/edu/classroom/answer/6386354?hl=en

Google Voice—https://voice.google.com/u/0/calls

Chapter 16
Technology Bootcamp

A great teacher can teach calculus with a paperclip and literature in an empty field. Technology is just another tool, not a destination.

—*Unknown*

I want to start by emphasizing the point made in this quote. Technology is merely a tool to help us facilitate teaching and learning. I don't believe technology will ever replace good teachers or solid pedagogy.

I believe that we need to understand how to use and leverage technology to help us save time, engage students, and meet individual learning needs without letting ourselves become complacent or using the technology as a crutch or replacement for teaching.

Understanding how to use and access these technology tools, however, becomes vitally important as we begin teaching/learning in a remote or hybrid environment. Teachers can't teach effectively if they don't understand their tools, students can't learn effectively if they can't access their work, and parents can't support their student if they don't understand the systems.

PSD Global Academy (PGA) Middle School starts each year with a "Technology Bootcamp" where students either learn, practice, or improve their understanding of the tools, systems, and platforms that will be essential for their learning over the course of the year.

Parents (learning coaches) are also required to complete portions of the bootcamp with their student, so we can ensure they know the systems well enough to assist their student on remote learning days.

The type of technology training or bootcamp the students engage in will be entirely dependent on the tools they will be expected to use and the skills they will need to complete tasks, which are often largely dictated by age.

Every year I have been surprised by what students do and don't know how to do. Things that seem obvious to us (sending an email, for example) are often entirely new to our students. We assume that because students can create a TikTok video, edit photos, or even write code they have comprehensive technical knowledge. But even the students who seem the most technically adept may never have been asked to complete a practical digital task, like using an online calendar or sharing a link. These are skills we must explicitly teach our students.

DIGITAL SKILLS BY GRADE

My Google Innovator cohort colleague, **Hans Tullmann**, crowd-sourced information from several teachers and technology leaders to understand which skills were most often required based on age or grade level. The following chart is an adaptation of that list.

K-1	2nd Grade	3rd-4th Grades	5th Grade
Turn devices on and off.	Use a browser to navigate the web.	Use presentation tools including i mages, video, and design.	Understand how to properly cite work using online citation tools.
Log in and out of an account.	Use keywords as search terms.	Type.	Type fluently.
Use a number of age-appropri-ate tools for learning (particularly touch-screen based with drag-and-drop functionality).	Use a word processing document for composition. Use a number of other age-appropriate tools for learning.	Understand how to share a document and collaborate or provide feedback to peers. Use a number of other age-appropriate tools for learning.	Send emails. Use a number of other age-appropriate tools for learning.

6th Grade	7th-8th Grade
Analyze the credibility of online sources.	Organize emails.
Take a screenshot.	Organize file storage.
Bookmark pages.	Organize calendar events.
Use keyboard shortcuts.	Use a spreadsheet.
Design a webpage.	Demonstrate design literacy.
Communicate professionally and/or appropriately online.	Demonstrate digital citizenship.

High School
All of the above
Using resources
Need-based media literacy

Kate Stevens, PGA high school educator and leader, recommends assessing your high schooler's technical abilities to see where they may have media literacy gaps that need to be addressed. She also teaches her students how to use their resources to fill those gaps themselves and seek out solutions for technical problems that may arise.

Stevens emphasizes that when teaching in a hybrid or blended environment, you are often teaching twice as much: the content as well as the digital tool. In speaking with me, she said, "If you aren't seeing the desired outcome on a piece of work, the medium you selected might not have been the right tool, or it might not have been taught correctly."

Stevens encourages all teachers to allow their students to practice and play in digital spaces before they are asked to create and have their learning assessed in them. If you are interested in learning more about digital standards, The International Society for Technology in Education has a **framework of technology standards** for both students and teachers, and many districts are adopting them as part of their curricula.

HOW TO TEACH DIGITAL SKILLS

Once you understand the skills and tools you want to teach your students, you need to determine a model for delivering the content.

At PGA middle school, we've created an entire Google Classroom for our technology bootcamps embedded with asynchronous lessons using Google Slides and Pear Deck for students to navigate independently.

Students have the entire first week of school to complete their asynchronous assignments on the "Pioneer 100" (aka Technology Bootcamp Google Classroom), while maintaining their regular class schedule. During live synchronous classes that week, teachers use the time to build culture and community, and support students as they work through these lessons. On asynchronous work days, teachers are in office hours to answer questions as well.

Structuring our first week of school this way is great in not only allowing us the time and space to teach technical and executive functioning skills and start building our relationships as a class but also to see which students are already struggling to complete asynchronous work and begin the appropriate interventions early.

If you are interested in creating a technology bootcamp to start your year or semester, here are my recommendations.

Create a Distinct Virtual Space for Your Technology Bootcamp

Whether it is a website, webpage, a Google Classroom, or other learning management system, the bootcamp should be delivered separately from any classwork your students will be engaging in.

Also, I recommend that you create a distinct space for your "bootcamp" that can also serve as an FAQ page or tech support site for students to revisit later in the year if they forget how to do something.

Look for Prebuilt Resources

Sometimes it's better to create resources and videos yourself, but if you have limited time and energy, you need to work smarter and not harder and head to YouTube to look for tutorials on the skills you want to teach.

Applied Digital Skills

Google's **Applied Digital Skills** program is a perfect example of a prebuilt resource (Figure 16.1). Applied Digital Skills is an entirely free online platform of video lessons that teaches digital and practical life skills. Lessons include how to "Track Due Dates and Tasks in Gmail," "Organize Files in Drive," "Send Professional Emails," and many, many more.

Figure 16.1: Applied Digital Skills lesson.

Applied Digital Skills was designed for students but could be easily used by teachers for their own professional development and even others who need to brush up on their own tech skills.

Applied Digital Skills also offers video lessons in Spanish and French.

As a Google product, it features only Google's own tools. So if your students use Microsoft Outlook rather than Gmail, you might have to look elsewhere (YouTube) for those tutorial videos.

Be Internet Awesome

Another free Google product that you might consider is **Be Internet Awesome**, a free curriculum to teach students about digital citizenship and online safety.

Be Internet Awesome has partnered with **Pear Deck** to provide premade Google Slides lessons, already embedded with interactive elements that teachers could use to teach digital citizenship live or assign asynchronously (student paced) to students.

Howdou

One of the products I am most excited about is being developed by my friends at **Canopy**. **Howdou** features interactive videos designed to help students learn by doing. They follow instructions within the video by clicking, typing, and navigating through tools like Google Classroom, Drive, Docs, and more (see Figure 16.2). The technology actually allows students to drive the process within the video as if they were on the tool itself.

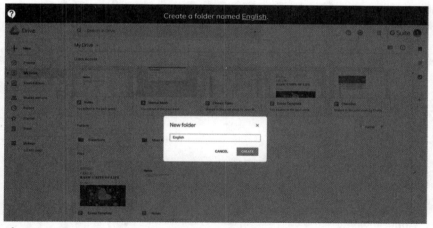

Figure 16.2: Howdou Google Drive lesson.

Howdou will give the student a summary of their performance, including suggestions for how to be more efficient in the future. The teacher will also be able to import students' scores directly into Google Classroom to monitor their work.

Students can collect "stamps" in a digital passport for each tool they master as a form of positive reinforcement.

You can try one yourself at https://www.canopy.education/skills.

Go Slow to Go Fast

As teachers, we are all probably familiar with the phrase "go slow to go fast." Typically it applies to the beginning of the year when we are establishing rules, norms, and routines that will help us set the framework for productive learning throughout the year. The same theory applies to teaching with technology.

Invest the time in the beginning of the year to make sure your students know how to use their tools before you set them to work. If your school or grade level implements Technology Bootcamp at the start of the year, you can save countless instructional minutes by not having to show each student where to click.

I recommend technology bootcamps for all schools that are using technology in their classrooms, whether they are traditional brick and mortar, hybrid, or online. Each school will need to look at the tools they have available to their students to determine what that bootcamp experience will look like and for whom it will be required.

RESOURCES

Items in **bold** in the text are listed here in the Resources. Direct access to all the following resources is available at https://hybridteacherresource.com and on this book's page on www.wiley.com.

Hans Tullmann's Twitter—https://twitter.com/HansTullmann

Kate Stevens' Twitter—https://twitter.com/KateTeaching

ISTE technology standards—https://www.iste.org/standards

Be Internet Awesome—https://beinternetawesome.withgoogle.com/en_us/

Pear Deck—https://www.peardeck.com/be-internet-awesome

Canopy—https://www.canopy.education

Howdou—https://www.howdou.net

Chapter 17
Teacher Time Savers

Work smarter, not harder.

—*Allan F. Mogensen*

I initially fell in love with educational technology for its ability to help me differentiate for and engage students, but I stayed in love with it for all the time it has saved me.

Good digital designers are always trying to create functions that require the fewest possible "clicks." Although a couple extra clicks of a mouse might not seem like that big of a deal, when you multiply those couple extra clicks by 180 students' work to grade or 180 days of the year, a few extra clicks becomes a lot of time.

The amount of time you can save in lesson planning, data assessment, and grading is well worth the investment of time to learn how to use these tools.

Here are my top tech time savers:

- ◆ Gmail Templates

  One of my best practices for student engagement during remote learning is to send immediate follow-up emails to students and their parents.
  Ideally, I will email a couple of students who did a great job engaging in
  the lessons, as well as all the students who were logged onto the video
  conferencing call, but didn't engage at all in the chat box or activity at all.

  Because I am writing this same email again and again, I use a **Gmail template**.
  Once the template has been created, all I have to do is click the "three
  dots" in the bottom corner of my email, then select the template title,
  and it autofills my email draft. (See Figure 17.1.)

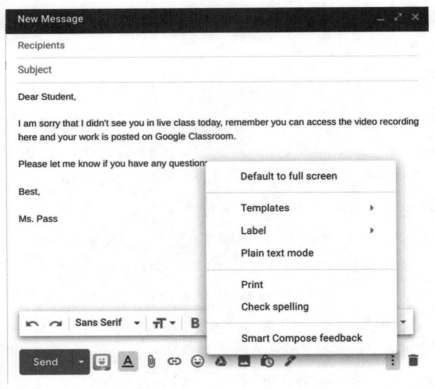

Figure 17.1: Gmail templates.

- Bookmarks

  Bookmarks are a fantastic way to keep track of every tool and resource you use on a regular or semi regular basis. Folders help you keep your bookmarks organized. My folders include EdTech Tools, Student Notes, Anchor Charts, To Do, etc.

  Not only can you bookmark websites, but you can bookmark your own Google Docs. I have several single-slide presentations bookmarked as "anchor charts," so if my students need a quick visual reminder on our class norms anchor chart/Google Slide or one on capitalization, I don't need to go searching through my Drive to find it; it's just a quick two clicks of a button away.

- Pinning Tabs

  Pretty much every document and website I use is bookmarked (plus many more I have yet to look at!), except for a few websites and documents that I use on a daily basis (my lesson planning template, email, attendance) I leave open in my browser all the time.

  Too many open tabs, however, create a little too much chaos in my browser, which is why I pin those daily use tabs, turning them from full-sized tabs to smaller, icon-only tabs that are fixed on the left-hand side of my browser. The other benefit to pinning tabs is that they must be unpinned before you can close them. So pinning your video conference will ensure you don't accidentally close out of it during class.

  To pin a tab, simply right click and select "pin."

  Super tech tip: If you shut off your computer regularly, leaving your Chrome Browser and pinned tabs open will ensure that next time you start your computer and open Chrome, your browser will bring those pinned tabs back up; or bookmarking all your pinned tabs in a folder called "Daily Pins" and right clicking the folder will allow you to "open all."

- Tab Groups

  If you are, indeed, the type of teacher who needs tons of tabs open at one time, organizing them by "tab group" can help you find what you are looking for quickly. Right click a tab, select "add tab to new group," and drag any other similar tab into the colored category. Repeat for additional tab groups.

This way, you can have a lesson planning tab group, a grading tab group, and an admin tab group open as you work.

◆ Starring Files

Similar to bookmarks and pins, putting a "star" on your folder or files in Google Drive makes them quick and easy to access. Right click the file or folder, then select "add to starred." I always "star" the folders for the current units we are working on, the roster lists, our weekly team meeting notes, and any lesson templates I am currently using. At the start of the next unit I will "un-star" the current files and repeat the process.

◆ File/Make a copy

In the previous item I mentioned that one of the things I like to "star" is lesson templates. I have a number of activities that I use regularly but change based on the content. Our vocabulary lesson, for example, is structured in a very similar way each time, with the same slide design and activity, but the vocabulary words change.

I have a template of the vocabulary lesson starred in my Drive, and any time a class does vocabulary, I go to the template and click "File" and "Make a copy," "entire presentation." Then all I have to do is change out the vocabulary words, save the new file in its correct folder with a new name, and post it to Google Classroom.

Lesson templates are particularly handy when I am doing a whole class collaborative doc activity (typically on Google Slides or Jamboard). In order for the activity to be successful, it helps to give each student their own slide or sticky note to work from.

At the beginning of the year I create a template with all the students' names on their own section, then any time I want to do a collaborative activity, I "File/make a copy" of that template (Figure 17.2), which saves me the time in typing each student's name from each class over and over again.

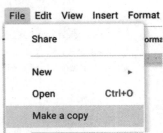

Figure 17.2: Make a copy in Google files.

"File/make a copy" is also great when reusing other teachers' lessons or HyperDocs (shared with permission) online.

◆ Google Classroom Grading Window

Of all the time-saving tools, Google Classroom Grading has probably saved me the most time of all.

Opening up a Google Doc or Slide assignment within Google Classroom allows you to preview a student's work, comment directly on the assignment, use a comment bank (accessed by the "#") to leave quick canned comments, score with or without a rubric, and best of all SCROLL on to the next student when you are done with the first.

I cannot emphasize the time saved in not having to open multiple links or sort through notebooks to find student work when you have a stack of nearly 200 papers to get through.

If Google Classroom is your learning management system, but not your gradebook, I still recommend grading and leaving feedback in Google Classroom, then splitting your screen to transfer the score over to your district's gradebook.

There are also many gradebook programs that have an automatic sync with Google Classroom. Check with your IT department to see if this applies to you.

◆ Google Forms to Sheets

There is so much I love about Google Forms (see Chapter 10, Attendance and Assessment), but it is one of my top time savers in the ability to export responses onto a Google Form.

Go to the "Responses" tab on a Google Form and look for the little green icon in the top right corner. This will allow you to export your answers either to a new Google Sheet or a new tab in an existing sheet.

Most often I use this feature either to quickly assess my entire class at a glance (great for "Do Nows" or "Exit Tickets") or to collect input from students. Ask students to contribute vocab words, questions, songs, or prompts and easily copy/paste their responses into your slide presentation.

- Version History

  In any Google Doc or Slide at the top right-hand side of your toolbar you'll see a notification that your "Last edit was..." and the ability to click that as a link.

  Because Google Docs are saved second by second, the file also creates a history of these changes that you can view by clicking that notification or going to "File" and "Version history."

  A column will open on the right-hand side of your file allowing you to see every day that file was worked on and for exactly how long.

  This is great for monitoring group work, because you can also see which user did which piece of work.

  As an English teacher, I use version history when I am grading final drafts. I simply look at the feedback I left on the first draft, click into the version history, and look to see if the new work meets the revision suggestions I left.

- Ctrl F

  "Control Find" is a keyboard shortcut. If you hold down the "Ctrl" and "F" keys at the same time, a text box will appear in the top right-hand side of your screen, regardless of the website or document you are on. From there you can search for any keyword, and as long as the webpage has text, Ctrl F will highlight and let you scroll to any instance of that search term appearing.

  I use this most often when I am trying to quickly find a parent email in our roster list, to find an assignment on Google Classroom, or to check to see if an article I am considering using covers the topic I am teaching.

- Google Docs Data

  In the top right-hand corner of your Google Docs, Slides, or Sheets (in a Google for Education account) you will see a little jagged arrow. That icon shows your document data. The most important item is who has viewed that file. You will see a list of every student who has opened the file and a time stamp of when they were on it. This allows you to quickly check which students have started their assignment and which students you need to give a gentle nudge.

RESOURCES

Items in **bold** in the text are listed here in the Resources. Direct access to the following resource is available at https://hybridteacherresource.com and on this book's page on www.wiley.com.

Gmail Template—https://support.google.com/a/users/answer/9308990?hl=en

Chapter 18
Going Further...

Live a life full of humility, gratitude, intellectual curiosity, and never stop learning.

—*Gza*

Learning is endless when it comes to education, let alone educational technology and remote or hybrid learning, and it is more than understandable if you are feeling overwhelmed. I always recommend teachers start by taking one thing they think they can implement in their classrooms, master that, then come back for the rest.

However, if you are ready to dig deeper beyond what is included in this book, here are some options to consider.

DEVELOP YOUR PERSONAL LEARNING NETWORK

A personal learning network (PLN) is a community of educators who share ideas, inspiration, encouragement, and resources with each other. Whether or not you feel like you have those colleagues in your department or school building, technology has made it easier than ever to connect with educators around the world and create a vibrant and diverse PLN.

- Twitter

    Twitter has long been the dominant social media site for educators to share and connect. Teachers and groups regularly host live "Twitter Chats" for teachers to engage in topics ranging from well-being to technology and everything in between.

    A **tutorial** on participating in Twitter chats if it is your first time is available at Youtube.com—search for Twitter Chat Basics.

Then, here are just a few of the amazing educators I recommend following on Twitter to get you started:

@emmabpass	@deelanier	@MrCaffrey	@abid_patel	@TrPatel20
@MsVenturino	@armstron-gedtech	@ShakeU-pLearning	@CheloELT	@Rachel_L_Dunne
@cogswell_ben	@mrpiercEy	@jmattmiller	@Steph_EdTech	@zbukhari197
@knikole	@burgessdave	@JNealeUK	@wterral	@TechMissC
@HollyC-larkEdu	@pernilleripp	@itbadger	@apsitnatasha	@mrshowell24
@trussleader-ship	@cultofpeda-gogy	@TomEMul-laney	@Ms_A_Yeh	@sdteaching
@mrsleban	@Catlin_Tucker	@ericcurts	@MissBeck-asaurus	@LesleighAlt-mann
@Simons_Darren	@k_shelton	@JakeMil-lerTech	@designed-schools	@Amber_A_Trout
@Rangathet-rainer	@paulmfarrell	@LisaBerghoff	@ClayCodes	@efitz_edtech
@CatLamin	@KimPolli-shuke	@edcampOSjr	@HansTull-mann	@meaganal-fano
@Devin-Rossiter	@pertuzluisfer	@EduFuturists	@Teacher_Luke_UK	@EdTechFor-ward

And so many more!

If you find me **@emmabpass** you can view all the teachers I follow. I recommend following every single one!

- Google Educator Groups

    If you are primarily using Google tools in your classroom, consider joining a **Google Educator Group (GEG)**. Many states or countries have their own groups, but you are not limited to your region and are free to join any or all groups if you'd like!

    Google for Education groups often hold free **professional development webinars** for their members and facilitate discussions on pedagogy with an emphasis on educational technology and Google tools.

- Other Social Media

    Twitter is by no means the only community of educators online! There are thriving professional learning networks for educators on Facebook, Instagram, Reddit, and TikTok (where I am increasingly learning about my favorite new tools!)

PROFESSIONAL DEVELOPMENT

Throughout this book I give suggestions on tools and techniques you may use within a hybrid, remote, or blended learning environment, but I give little instruction on how to actually use them. However, there are plenty of resources to help provide that additional, tool-specific instruction.

- YouTube

    YouTube is my go-to for any EdTech tutorial. If an educator has used a tool to teach, there is a good chance there is also a video tutorial for it on YouTube. Most of my EdTech learning has been self-directed through YouTube tutorials. If you are self-motivated, you can do a lot of the learning there for free!

- **Empowered Edu**

    If you prefer a more structured or in-person learning experience, you could consider hiring a consultant to lead a training for your department, school, or district.

My consultancy, Empowered Edu LLC, offers education technology training and consulting, including a public remote, synchronous training, asynchronous video training, and bespoke sessions for schools and districts.

EMPOWERED edu

Visit my site (edtechemma.com/pd) for more information on how to work with me to deliver training for the teachers in your school, district, or department.

- EdTech Companies

  Most EdTech companies provide live training or training videos on their own tools and products. Check their websites and YouTube channels to find out.

- Local EdTech Leaders

  Chances are there are already some amazing educators in your school or district who can provide a lot of valuable training and insight.

  Don't overlook the experts in your own backyard, because they'll often understand your student population, technology access, and tools, as well as your potential challenges and limitations better than any outside trainer.

GET A BADGE

Now that you are developing all of your EdTech skills, you might as well have something to show for it! Several companies offer badges that you can earn for completing their programs or assessments.

- **Google Certified Educator**

  Google offers a badge for Educator Level 1 and 2, Trainer, Coach, and Innovator (Figure 18.1). The Educator Badges require a timed, skill-based exam; whereas the Trainer and Coach badges require completing a number of training hours and submitting examples of your work.

  There is typically a small fee to take your badge exam.

  Google Certified Innovator is a truly special program that accepts a small cohort of educators a few times a year to participate in a free

Figure 18.1: Google for Education badges.

three-day program at a Google Office somewhere in the United States or internationally (I attended with a cohort in London, but locations are always changing).

Through the program you are coached and mentored as you complete a project over the course of the following year. **It is an inspiring and career-changing experience.** I encourage everyone to apply.

- **Apple Education**

  Apple offers an Apple Teacher badge through a free, self-paced online program focused on teaching through the use of Apple hardware like iPads and Macbooks.

- **Microsoft Education**

  Microsoft offers a number of badges, one for each of their tools or skills. You can earn an Office 365 Badge, a OneNote badge, or an Inclusive Classroom badge, to name a few.

  The courses to obtain these badges are typically shorter than most programs and free to complete.

- More!

  EdTech badges don't stop there. Rachael Coathup, Google Certified Innovator and primary school teacher in the United Kingdom, has developed a handy website called **BadgEdTech** to help teachers and students access resources for a number of different educational badges, certificates, and accreditation.

Badges are fun in and of themselves, but they can also look really good on a resume if you are applying for future positions that require knowledge of educational technology.

ADDITIONAL READING AND RESOURCES

If you are more of the reading type, here are some of my favorite blogs and books for educational technology and blended learning:

- **EdTechEmma**—My own blog, I think you already have a good sense of the type of content I write about!

- **Cult of Pedagogy**—Written and curated by Jennifer Gonzalez and a team, tackles the whole spectrum of issues in education, but often discusses the use of technology.

- **Catlin Tucker**—High school English teacher and the author of several books, she shares lots of great tips from her classroom, many of which include the use of technology.

- **Ditch That Textbook**—Matt Miller and team are always cranking out loads of great curated EdTech resources for classroom teachers.

- **Shake Up Learning**—Kasey Bell has plenty of great, quick tutorials. She often comes up first when I do a Google search of a technical issue I've run into.

- **The Perfect Blend**—Michelle Eaton uses her experience as an online teacher and instructional designer to share great tips and strategies for incorporating a blended learning model into the classroom.

ESSENTIAL EdTech TOOL BOX

In this book I mention how I use several EdTech tools in my lessons, but I don't necessarily explain all the features. You can find step-by-step tutorials on the websites in the following table or on YouTube.

EdTech Tool	Description	Additional Resources
Google Classroom	Learning management system	**Video Tutorial**
Google Sites	Simple website design platform	**Video Tutorial**
Applied Digital Skills	Video-based, asynchronous lessons	**Getting Started**
Google Slides	Presentation and design tool	**Video Tutorial**
Quizizz	Review-style online game	**Video Tutorial**
Google Forms	Quiz and survey tool	**Video Tutorial**
Jamboard	Online, collaborative whiteboard	**What is Jamboard?**

EdTech Tool	Description	Additional Resources
Flipgrid	Video discussion tool	**Video Tutorial**
Padlet	Online, collaborative discussion tool	**Video Tutorial**
Google Meet	Video conferencing tool	**Training and Help**
Flippity	Google Sheet game tool	**Video Tutorial**
Quizlet	Digital flash card review	**Teacher Guide**
Google Expeditions	Virtual reality tours	**Getting Started**
GoNoodle	Movement videos	**10 Ways to GoNoodle**
Pear Deck	Interactive presentation tool	**Training**
Parlay	Online discussion tool	**Facilitate Discussion**
Screencastify	Screen recording tool	**Beginner's Guide**
Edpuzzle	Interactive video lessons	**Video Tutorial**
Hyperdocs	Digital lesson templates	**How Hyperdocs Transform**
GoFormative	Online assessment tool	**Video Tutorial**
Seesaw	Learning management system	**YouTube Channel**
Canva	Graphic design tool	**Canva for Classroom Course**
Google Forms Escape Room	Teacher-created digital escape rooms.	**Forms Escape Room Tutorial**

RESOURCES

Items in **bold** in the text are listed here in the Resources. Direct access to all the following resources is available at https://hybridteacherresource.com and on this book's page on www.wiley.com.

Twitter Chat Tutorial—https://www.youtube.com/watch?v=q0OYSwAz8J8

Twitter Profiles:

Emma B. Pass's Twitter—https://twitter.com/emmabpass

Mari Venturino's Twitter—https://twitter.com/MsVenturino

Ben Cogswell's Twitter—https://twitter.com/cogswell_ben

Knikole Taylor's Twitter—https://twitter.com/knikole

Holly Clark's Twitter—https://twitter.com/HollyClarkEdu

Joe Truss's Twitter—https://twitter.com/trussleadership

Jennifer Leban's Twitter—https://twitter.com/mrsleban

Darren Simons' Twitter—https://twitter.com/Simons_Darren

MyEdTechBuddy's Twitter—https://twitter.com/Rangathetrainer

Cat Lamin's Twitter—https://twitter.com/CatLamin

Devin Rossiter's Twitter—https://twitter.com/DevinRossiter

Dee Lanier's Twitter—https://twitter.com/deelanier

Michelle Armstrong's Twitter—https://twitter.com/armstrongedtech

Donnie Piercey's Twitter—https://twitter.com/mrpiercEy

Dave Burgess's Twitter—https://twitter.com/burgessdave

Pernille Ripp's Twitter—https://twitter.com/pernilleripp

Jennifer Gonzalez's Twitter—https://twitter.com/cultofpedagogy

Catlin Tucker's Twitter—https://twitter.com/Catlin_Tucker

Ken Shelton's Twitter—https://twitter.com/k_shelton

Paul Farrell's Twitter—https://twitter.com/paulmfarrell

Kim Pollishuke's Twitter—https://twitter.com/KimPollishuke

Luis Fernando Pertuz Escribano's Twitter—https://twitter.com/pertuzluisfer

Andrew Caffrey's Twitter—https://twitter.com/MrCaffrey

Kasey Bell's Twitter—https://twitter.com/ShakeUpLearning

Matt Miller's Twitter—https://twitter.com/jmattmiller

Jon Neale's Twitter—https://twitter.com/JNealeUK

Dave Leonard's Twitter—https://twitter.com/itbadger

Tom Mullaney's Twitter—https://twitter.com/TomEMullaney

Eric Curts's Twitter—https://twitter.com/ericcurts

Jake Miller's Twitter—https://twitter.com/JakeMillerTech

Lisa Berghoff's Twitter—https://twitter.com/LisaBerghoff

Ed Campos Jr.'s Twitter—https://twitter.com/edcampOSjr

Edufuturists' Twitter—https://twitter.com/EduFuturists

Abid Patel's Twitter—https://twitter.com/abid_patel

Chelo Gutiérrez's Twitter—https://twitter.com/CheloELT

Stephanie Rothstein's Twitter—https://twitter.com/Steph_EdTech

Wanda Terral's Twitter—https://twitter.com/wterral

Natasha Rachell's Twitter—https://twitter.com/apsitnatasha

Aubrey Yeh's Twitter—https://twitter.com/Ms_A_Yeh

Becky Unger Shorey's Twitter—https://twitter.com/MissBeckasaurus

Lauren Heil's Twitter—https://twitter.com/designedschools

Clay Smith's Twitter—https://twitter.com/ClayCodes

Hans Tullmann's Twitter—https://twitter.com/HansTullmann

Luke Craig's Twitter—https://twitter.com/Teacher_Luke_UK

Sonal Patel's Twitter—https://twitter.com/TrPatel20

Rachel Dunne's Twitter—https://twitter.com/Rachel_L_Dunne

Z Bukhari's Twitter—https://twitter.com/zbukhari197

Rachel Coathup's Twitter—https://twitter.com/TechMissC

Stephanie Howell's Twitter—https://twitter.com/mrshowell24

Eric Cross's Twitter—https://twitter.com/sdteaching

Lesleigh Altmann's Twitter—https://twitter.com/LesleighAltmann

Amber Trout's Twitter—https://twitter.com/AmberPearDeck

Emily Fitzpatrick's Twitter—https://twitter.com/efitz_edtech

Meagan Alfano's Twitter—https://twitter.com/meaganalfano

Kris Armijo's Twitter—https://twitter.com/EdTechForward

Google Educator Groups (GEG)—https://teachercenter.withgoogle.com/communities

Global Google Educator Group PD Webinars—https://www.youtube.com/channel/UCkBXjjUuce3SgqtVD-EbHFA

EmpoweredEdu—https://www.edtechemma.com/shop

Google Certified Educator—https://teachercenter.withgoogle.com/certification_level1

Google Certified Innovator—https://edu.google.com/teacher-center/programs/certified-innovator/?modal_active=none

"5 Things I Learned at Google Certified Innovator Academy"—https://www.edtechemma.com/single-post/2019/08/11/5-Things-I-Learned-at-Google-Certified-Innovator-Academy

Apple Education—https://www.apple.com/education/k12/apple-teacher/

Microsoft Education—https://education.microsoft.com/en-us

BadgEdTech—https://sites.google.com/view/badgedtech/home?authuser=0

EdTechEmma—https://www.edtechemma.com/blog

Cult of Pedagogy—https://www.cultofpedagogy.com

Catlin Tucker's Website—https://catlintucker.com

Ditch That Textbook—https://ditchthattextbook.com

Shake Up Learning—https://shakeuplearning.com

"The Perfect Blend" by Michelle Eaton—https://www.thriftbooks.com/w/the-perfect-blend-a-practical-guide-to-designing-student-centered-learning-experiences_michele-eaton/25861511/item/38568064/

EdTech Tools and Additional Resources:

Google Classroom—https://classroom.google.com/u/0/h

Google Classroom Video Tutorial—https://www.youtube.com/watch?v=a2O5ce_Y99A

Google Sites—https://sites.google.com/new

Google Sites Video Tutorial—https://www.youtube.com/watch?v=n-0O2ZOIpZA

Applied Digital Skills—https://applieddigitalskills.withgoogle.com/s/en/home?test=1&utm_expid=.Wm-fQSUHTxa4Fqvc8R48kg.1&utm_referrer=https%3A%2F%2Fwww.google.com%2F

Getting Started with Applied Digital Skills—https://grow.google/programs/app-skills/

Google Slides—https://www.google.com/slides/about/

Google Slides Video Tutorial—https://www.youtube.com/watch?v=BsMuKfNvA50&t=242s

Quizizz—https://quizizz.com

Quizizz Video Tutorial—https://www.youtube.com/watch?v=oDO3j2PjS7s

Google Forms—https://www.google.com/forms/about/

Google Forms Video Tutorial—https://www.youtube.com/watch?v=LLSzalIY5_s&t=2s

Jamboard—https://jamboard.google.com

What is Jamboard?—https://www.edtechemma.com/single-post/2018/11/05/The-Jamboard-Series-Part-I---What-is-Google-Jamboard

Flipgrid—https://info.flipgrid.com

Flipgrid Video Tutorial—https://www.youtube.com/watch?v=Jn9zvfd3niM

Padlet—http://padlet.com

Padlet Video Tutorial—https://www.youtube.com/watch?v=OPkq5q8nRbM

Google Meet—https://meet.google.com

Google Meet Training and Help—https://support.google.com/a/users/answer/9282720?hl=en

Flippity—https://flippity.net

Flippity Video Tutorial—https://www.youtube.com/watch?v=OOd3pwHhbt8

Quizlet—https://quizlet.com

Quizlet Teacher Guide—https://quizlet.com/features/quizlet-teacher-guide-getting-started

Google Expeditions—https://edu.google.com/products/vr-ar/expeditions/?modal_active=none

Getting Started with Google Expeditions—http://mrcaffrey.com/google-expeditions/

GoNoodle—https://www.gonoodle.com

10 Ways to GoNoodle—https://www.gonoodle.com/blog/10-ways-to-gonoodle-for-beginners/

Pear Deck—https://www.peardeck.com

Pear Deck Training—https://www.peardeck.com/learn-pear-deck

Parlay—https://parlayideas.com

Facilitate Discussions with Parlay—https://www.edtechemma.com/single-post/2020/04/12/Parlay---The-Best-Way-to-Facilitate-Online-Class-Discussions

Screencastify—https://www.screencastify.com

Beginner's Guide to Screencastify—https://www.screencastify.com/blog/beginners-guide-educators

Edpuzzle—http://edpuzzle.com

Edpuzzle Video Tutorial—https://www.youtube.com/watch?v=gnL1DsRAQ0E

HyperDocs—https://www.hyperdocs.co

How HyperDocs Transform—https://www.cultofpedagogy.com/hyperdocs/

GoFormative—https://goformative.com

GoFormative Video Tutorial—https://www.youtube.com/watch?v=DrKcmtBXlfY

Seesaw—https://web.seesaw.me

Seesaw Youtube Channel—https://www.youtube.com/channel/UCYUfn-b7MIsGald-Xtig9Umw

Canva—https://www.canva.com/education/

Canva for the Classroom Course— https://designschool.canva.com/courses/canva-for-the-classroom/?lesson=build-design-literacy

Google Forms Escape Room Tutorial—https://www.bespokeclassroom.com/blog/2019/10/4/how-to-build-a-digital-escape-room-using-google-forms

Chapter 19
The Future of Education Is Hybrid

Education is not only a ladder of opportunity, but it is also an investment in our future.

—Ed Markey

When the COVID-19 dust settles and we reflect on what we've learned, I hope we realize the power of technology in education and the potential for hybrid and blended learning.

Hybrid and remote education could become an integral part of traditional school systems, not only by providing uninterrupted education during snow days, natural disasters, and pandemics but also as a viable model of education for rural students, those who are homebound, and as "schools-of-choice" for all types of students.

The biggest drawback with the hybrid model is the dependence on a parent or guardian who is able to support a student's remote learning from home, which obviously leaves out the majority of the students in our country who have working parents.

I also envision a hybrid school where students would still have the option of being on campus every day.

I imagine a school where students' schedules are need based. The students who need more direction and support might participate in live classes or small tutor groups all day. The students who are able, and prefer having more independence, have some live classes they attend and then have the option to do their additional work from home or in a communal school space that is monitored by support staff, who can keep the students on task and safe.

In this model, teachers will play a smaller role in the "monitoring" of students and have more time to devote to curriculum design, lesson planning, assessment, and intervention.

I believe there is potential to build a more equitable school system using technology, remote instruction, and student-driven learning, so that the students who have the greatest needs are given the time and attention they deserve, and the students who are self-sufficient are allowed to be so.

WHAT DID I MISS?

As I mentioned in the introduction, I wrote this book from a very specific lens, and based on my own experience I recognize there will be many people who see things differently than I do.

If you have any feedback for me, I would truly appreciate hearing from you.

Feedback is accepted on a Google Form that can be found at bit.ly/hybridteacherfeedback.

TAKE CARE

Last, but certainly not least, remember that learning is never finished. Whether you are using educational technology for the first time or have been teaching online for years, there is always more to know.

Take comfort in the knowledge that you will never know it all, and remember to take care of your physical, mental, and emotional well-being. Take good care of yourself in order to take good care of our kids. You can do it.

Teach on,
Emma Pass

Chapter 20
The Administrators' Appendix

A great opera house isn't run by a director, but by a great administrator.
—Steven Berkoff

The majority of this book was written for classroom teachers, but for administrators either implementing elements of a hybrid model in their school as a plan for emergency response, or interested in the greater potential of hybrid learning for the future, the following sections include general information on hybrid education.

WHAT IS HYBRID LEARNING?

Although hybrid schools have been around for more than a decade, the concept is still relatively new and unknown to most. When I applied for my current position at PGA, even I didn't know what a hybrid school was.

Essentially, a hybrid school combines traditional in-person, brick-and-mortar education with online learning. The "hybrid" component refers to a physical environment that blends in-person and remote (at-home) learning.

Every hybrid school approaches this combination differently. The amount of time students are spending in the building vs learning at home/online will vary from school to school, as will the nature and pacing of online resources.

For example, some hybrid schools will purchase prebuilt online curricula, whereas others will rely upon the teachers themselves to build virtual content. Some hybrid schools will give students access to the entire semester's worth of work from the first day, and others will release content on a daily or weekly basis. Some hybrid schools are a part of the public school district, whereas others are private or charter schools.

For many, the first time they've heard of hybrid learning was during the response to COVID-19, when many brick-and-mortar schools elected to adopt hybrid models to reduce the amount of students in person at any given time. It's important to note that these were **emergency hybrid models** and are not representative of the quality and potential of hybrid learning as a whole.

The most common COVID emergency hybrid models group students and alternate days on campus during the week, as the model in Figure 20.1 shows.

Although hybrid schools were virtually unheard of before the COVID-19 pandemic, we may see hybrid models become a permanent part of school districts around the country in the future.

	Monday	Tuesday	Wednesday	Thursday	Friday
Group A	On Site	Remote	High Needs Students— On Site	On Site	Remote
Group B	Remote	On Site	Others— Remote / Teacher Plan	Remote	On Site

Figure 20.1: COVID response hybrid model.

I also believe blended, remote, and asynchronous learning strategies will become a more common component of traditional brick-and-mortar schools for a variety of reasons: instruction can be delivered on snow days; students who are sick or homebound can join school virtually, or watch recordings of lessons; and parent communication can be delivered in person or virtually, based on individual need.

WHY HYBRID LEARNING?

What type of student chooses a hybrid school? I genuinely couldn't predict what the student population would look like before I started working at PGA, but what I found, of course, is that there are a wide variety of students who chose hybrid learning for a number of reasons.

Our PGA students:

- wanted smaller learning communities and closer relationships with their teachers and peers.
- have been previously homeschooled and have parents who enjoy more involvement in their child's education.
- have extracurricular hobbies/careers that they are pursuing (elite athletics, music, businesses) and need a more flexible schedule
- cope with social anxiety and have a hard time attending school five days/week.
- have medical conditions that often mean they are in the hospital or homebound for long stretches of time.
- are teen parents.
- want more control of their learning.

Whatever the reason, a hybrid school works well for some students and not as well for others. In my experience, the hybrid model tends to work best for students who:

- need more flexibility in the pace of their learning.
  - Those who need more time to complete their work, or who can complete work more quickly than their peers, are allowed that flexibility when working asynchronously/remotely. They aren't confined to the pace of the "average."

- are highly self-motivated or have a parent/guardian at home who holds them accountable for doing their work.
- are organized or have a parent/guardian at home who is able to help them stay organized and prioritize their time.
- are naturally more introverted and enjoy being at home for a greater percentage of their week.

These are the ideal qualities of a hybrid school student. In reality, very few of our students have all of these characteristics. In fact, there are some students at PGA who have none of the above but still thrive in our environment for one reason or another.

Ultimately, it is hard to predict with 100% confidence which students will do well and which won't. In our school it is a trial-and-error process where we are continually evaluating which students are doing well, and which require more support.

As we've already seen, the hybrid model works better for some students than others. When it works, there are plenty of benefits:

- Students are able to work at a pace that suits their learning style.
- Parents are more invested and involved in their student's education.
- Students build digital skills.
- Students build executive functioning skills.
- Some teachers have more time to properly prepare lessons and assess learning.
- There are more opportunities to work with small groups or have smaller class sizes.
- There is greater flexibility if students and/or teachers can't make it to school.
- School building operating expenses may be reduced.

THE HYBRID TEACHER

No matter the model, teaching in a hybrid environment will be an adjustment for teachers who are accustomed to a traditional school, particularly on days when the students are working and learning from home.

In my experience, hybrid teaching:

- requires a more comprehensive understanding of the tools and technology that can help facilitate online learning, discussion, assessment, and community.

- takes thoughtful planning to determine which activities are better suited for an in-person day vs which can be completed more easily asynchronously or online.

- is more difficult to hold students accountable for doing their work when they are online and requires teachers to stay current on grading so that they will notice when a student has disengaged.

- requires creativity in adapting lessons and activities that have been designed for a traditional classroom environment.

- requires greater communication and partnership with parents/learning coaches.

Still, I love it.

The time I get to plan, grade, and communicate with individual students while they are learning asynchronously/remotely is a gift that I didn't realize was possible in education. I treasure the relationships I have with my students and colleagues. Our school might be small and a little unusual, but our community is big and bright.

What I wish I knew before I started hybrid teaching:

- Staying organized in how you post your work and communicate with your students is key to their academic success.

- Cohesive and consistent systems among classes/colleagues help students navigate the online environment.

- Students and parents have communication preferences. Ask them how they'd like to communicate with you (text, email, Google Classroom) and they'll be more likely to respond.

- The amount of time available to complete a task is the amount of time it will take. If I give myself all day to plan a lesson, it will take all day. If I give myself an hour, it will take (just a little more than) an hour. Use timers to help you manage your time, and teach students to do the same.
- Students are adaptable and resilient—don't underestimate them.
- You are adaptable and resilient—don't underestimate yourself.

TRADITIONAL HYBRID SCHOOL EXAMPLES

The basic premise of hybrid learning is always the same, in that time is divided between campus and home; however, hybrid schools vary greatly in how they organize that time. The following are a few examples of different models.

PSD Global Academy—Fort Collins, Colorado

At **PSD Global Academy (PGA)**, we group our school into three distinct teams/ schools: elementary (K-5), middle (6-8), and high (9-12). Although we all share the same building, attend all-school staff meetings, and collaborate with each other, each school has a different schedule and system of operation that meets the needs of that developmental age.

Elementary School (K-5):

Monday	Tuesday	Wednesday	Thursday	Friday
Remote	On Campus	Remote	On Campus	Remote

Remote/Online Learning Days

The students:	The teacher:
On these days the elementary students stay at home and complete their learning. Their "learning coach" acts as the primary teacher who will teach the content and lead their child through educational exercises and activities. The lessons are created by the classroom teacher and posted for the parents/learning coaches to access on a learning management system (LMS). The classroom teacher is also available via phone/email/video to answer questions as they arise throughout the school day.	The classroom teacher is typically lesson planning, grading, and talking with students/ parents over email, phone, or video confer- ences on these days as needed.

On-Campus Days

The students:	The teacher:
On these days the students come to the school building and engage in a traditional education model. They spend the majority of their day in the classroom with their classroom teacher but also attend extracurricular classes including physical education, music, and art.	The classroom teacher is leading all classroom instruction.

Middle School (6-8):

Monday	Tuesday	Wednesday	Thursday	Friday
Remote	On Campus	On Campus + Remote	On Campus	Remote

Remote/Online Learning Days

The students:	The teacher:
On these days the middle school students stay at home and complete their learning independently with their "learning coach" in a support versus teaching role. All lessons are created by the classroom teachers and posted for the student to access on an LMS. Direct instruction is often delivered via video on these days, either prerecorded or via live video conferencing.	The classroom teacher is typically lesson planning, grading, and talking with students/ parents over email, phone, or video confer- ences on these days.

On-Campus Days

The students:	The teachers:
On these days, the students come to the school building and engage in a traditional education model.	The classroom teachers are leading all classroom instruction.
They spend their day in 60-minute block periods and move from classroom to classroom as they attend math, science, language arts, physical education, and either art or music.	
Language arts and math are in 2-hour blocks; one is scheduled as a regular class and one is called "What I Need" or WIN, which focuses on intervention and enrichment.	

Wednesday Open Lab

The students:	The teachers:
On Wednesday mornings from 8:20-11:20, students have the option to come to campus for "open lab" where they can spend their time working independently on their online work, work with classmates, or receive small group or 1-1 tutoring from their teachers.	The classroom teachers spend open lab working with individual or small groups of students and monitoring student work and behavior to make sure students stay on-task.
There is also an optional "history lab" on Wednesdays, where students can choose to engage in a hands-on history project rather than doing their online history assignment for that day.	After open lab, each teacher is responsible for facilitating or supervising a club.
At 11:20 students can be picked up by their parents/learning coaches and go home to complete the remainder of their work for that day, or they can stay on campus for clubs. Some of our clubs include Science Bowl, Dungeon & Dragons, Gameboard Club, and Mathletes. Some of the clubs are led by teachers and others are student led and organized.	When the students leave, all middle school teachers (and the principal) meet for weekly collaboration and kid-talk time.
Wednesday Open Lab is optional but encouraged.	

High School (9-12):

Monday	Tuesday	Wednesday	Thursday	Friday
On Campus	Remote	On Campus	On Campus	Remote

Remote/Online Learning Days

The students:	The teacher:
On these days the high school students stay at home and complete their learning independently. All lessons are created by the classroom teachers and posted for the student to access on an LMS. Direct instruction is often delivered via video on these days, either prerecorded or via live video call.	The classroom teacher is typically lesson planning, grading, and talking with students over email, phone, or video conferences on these days.

On-Campus Days

The students:	The teachers:
On these days the students come to the school building and will either be in a live class or in "flex lab" depending on their schedule for that day. Live classes are 90-minute block periods that typically occur twice a week. If a student is not scheduled to be in class, they go to "flex lab" (in our gym/cafeteria) where they can work on their online/asynchronous lessons or receive tutoring or small-group instruction.	The classroom teachers are either leading live class instruction or monitoring "flex lab." Teachers in "flex lab" often pull individual or small groups of students for intervention or enrichment work.

Springs Studio—Colorado Springs, Colorado

Springs Studio is also a K-12 public hybrid school. It operates on a similar weekly schedule model in which each grade level is on campus 2–3 days/week and learning remotely 2–3 days/week.

My colleagues and I had the opportunity to visit Springs Studio in 2019 and speak with their principal and staff about the model they've adopted for their school (Figure 20.2).

SSAE HIGH SCHOOL WEEKLY SCHEDULE

	Monday	Tuesday	Wednesday	Thursday	Friday
Where	SSAE CAMPUS	Home	SSAE CAMPUS	Home	SSAE CAMPUS
Morning	Direct Instruction On Campus *Blended Students Required to Attend Classes	All Student Virtual Day *Teachers Accessible through Zoom Conferencing	Direct Instruction On Campus *Blended Students Required to Attend Classes	All Student Virtual Day *Teachers Accessible through Zoom Conferencing	Content Specific Student Support Labs and Interventions *Virtual Day for Students who do not require interventions
Lunch	Lunch		Lunch		Lunch
Afternoon	Direct Instruction On Campus *Blended Students Required to Attend Classes		Direct Instruction On Campus *Blended Students Required to Attend Classes		No Students on Campus

Figure 20.2: Springs Studio hybrid model 2019/2020.

One of the major differences between PGA and Springs Studio is that PGA teachers are responsible for 100% of the curriculum and content creation, whereas Springs Studio teachers use a prebuilt online curriculum (purchased from a third-party company) for remote-learning days. This approach enables them to focus on more project-based and high-engagement learning during their on-campus days.

Also, Springs Studio makes the entire semester's worth of content available to students on the first day; in contrast, PGA releases remote/asynchronous content on a daily or weekly basis.

There is no right or wrong way to organize hybrid learning, but it is always valuable to see what others are doing to determine how to best support your student population.

COVID-19 HYBRID MODELS

In response to COVID-19, many brick-and-mortar schools elected to adopt hybrid models to reduce the amount of students in-person at any given time.

It is important to note that, in most cases, these solutions will **not be typical hybrid models**. Similarly, the remote learning many of us engaged in this past spring was **not typical of remote learning**.

Schools were in an emergency scenario. The proper time, funding, and training had not been provided to teachers and schools to facilitate optimal hybrid and remote learning.

If, based on your experience of remote learning during the pandemic, you believe that remote or hybrid learning "doesn't work" or that hybrid learning is "less effective," please keep an open mind about hybrid learning in an **ideal scenario**.

I agree that what many schools needed to do in 2020—"emergency remote learning"—is likely less effective than traditional models we've had centuries to refine.

With that in mind, the following sections present a few examples of hybrid models that schools adopted in order to address the COVID-19 pandemic and reduce class sizes enough to meet social distancing requirements.

The most common solution involves breaking students into groups for alternating sessions of on-campus and remote instruction.

Model 1: Alternating Groups Within the Week

These schools had a Monday/Thursday group and a Tuesday/Friday group. When one group was on campus, the other was learning remotely/at home, and vice versa.

In this example, I've also reserved Wednesday for the highest-need students to come to campus to receive targeted intervention, while the other students work remotely, as well as provide teachers with additional plan time. (See Figure 20.3.)

	Monday	Tuesday	Wednesday	Thursday	Friday
Group A	On Site	Remote	High Needs Students— On Site	On Site	Remote
			Others— Remote		
Group B	Remote	On Site	Teacher Plan	Remote	On Site

Figure 20.3: COVID response hybrid model: alternating days within the week, Monday/Thursday and Tuesday/Friday groups.

The benefit of this model is that students are staying actively engaged with their school, the culture, the community, and their peers.

The difficulty is in the workload of the teacher, who is responsible for facilitating on-campus and remote instruction at the same time.

Some schools adopted variations of this model, where students' on-site days were chunked at the beginning or end of the week (Figure 20.4).

Or, without the Wednesday for intervention and plan time, some schools had an alternating M/W/F and T/TH schedule, as shown in Figure 20.5.

Model 2: Alternating Groups Based on the Week

In this model, there is a Week A and a Week B. Students alternate between weeks of on-campus and remote learning (Figure 20.6).

	Monday	Tuesday	Wednesday	Thursday	Friday
Group A	Remote	Remote	High Needs Students—On Site	On Site	On Site
Group B	On Site	On Site	Others—Remote Teacher Plan	Remote	Remote

Figure 20.4: COVID response hybrid model: alternating days within the week, Monday/Tuesday and Thursday/Friday groups.

Week 1

	Monday	Tuesday	Wednesday	Thursday	Friday
Group A	On Site	Remote	On Site	Remote	On Site
Group B	Remote	On Site	Remote	On Site	Remote

Week 2

	Monday	Tuesday	Wednesday	Thursday	Friday
Group A	Remote	On Site	Remote	On Site	Remote
Group B	On Site	Remote	On Site	Remote	On Site

Figure 20.5: COVID response hybrid model: alternating days within the week, alternating Wednesdays.

	Week 1	Week 2
Group A	On Site	Remote
Group B	Remote	On Site

Figure 20.6: COVID response hybrid model: alternating weeks.

Of note, this model may have further mitigated the spread of disease between groups, as deep cleaning could be performed on weekends, and the duration of the weekend itself may have allowed for greater evacuation of airborne coronavirus particles.

This model also allows for longer stretches of in-depth, in-person learning.

The difficulty is in keeping the students engaged at home for an entire week of remote/limited contact.

Model 3: Alternating Groups by Half Days

Some schools asked all students to come to the building every day for a half day, with cleaning between groups of students. In this model, there is a morning group and an afternoon group that stays consistent, or "A" and "B" groups that alternate which days of the week they attend school in the morning and afternoon (Figure 20.7).

The benefit of this half-day model is that kids are connecting with their teachers and peers in person every day. It also eliminates the need for students to eat on campus. Students who rely on free/reduced lunch could take sack lunches home for that afternoon and/or the next day (depending on their schedule), so students wouldn't need to eat on campus at all.

The difficulty is in properly cleaning and sanitizing the building every day between groups, and the increased strain on transportation when school buses also need to limit their capacity.

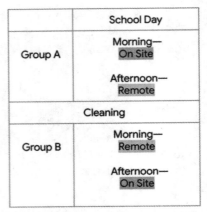

	School Day
Group A	Morning— On Site
	Afternoon— Remote
Cleaning	
Group B	Morning— Remote
	Afternoon— On Site

Figure 20.7: COVID response hybrid model: alternating within the day.

Model 4: High-Needs Students Only

Another model is having only the highest-need students back on campus and asking the students who have the resources to do so (including technology and parental support) to continue remote learning from home.

Those highest-need students might consist of our littlest learners (pre K-2), special education students, English language learners, students of essential workers, and any other student who isn't able to learn from home.

ALTERNATING, COORDINATED, AND CONCURRENT INSTRUCTION

In this book, we've explored synchronous and asynchronous instruction models, both of which I believe play an important role in a well-balanced education.

Bring it back to the building

Although it might seem like the need for these models will disappear when the pandemic is over, there are always reasons why some of our students don't make it to class on any given day and could benefit from an established strategy for participating in their learning from home.

In a full-time brick-and-mortar school, teachers who have students in the classroom 5 days each week might choose to make one or two lessons entirely asynchronous, for students to work through in the classroom independently (with assistance from the teacher).

Established hybrid schools often have students working asynchronously on their remote days and engage in synchronous lessons when they are on campus.

However, during COVID-19 we saw the need to have two groups of students: one in the classroom, one remote. Because of that, each school had to decide how each group of students would be engaging in their learning, resulting in the three models shown here.

- **Alternating Instruction**

    The first option would be to alternate lessons. For instance, for Monday/Tuesday, you would have one asynchronous lesson plan for your remote students and one synchronous lesson plan for your students on campus. These lessons would complement each other and could be delivered in either order. The students who complete the remote/asynchronous lesson on Monday would have the on-campus/synchronous lesson on Tuesday, and vice versa (see Figure 20.8).

- **Coordinated Instruction**

    In this option you would have two versions of your Monday lesson plan; one that could be delivered on campus and one that has already been recorded and can be watched remotely/asynchronously.

    This would require much more planning, but you'd benefit from being able to collaborate with the students who are at home that day during class.

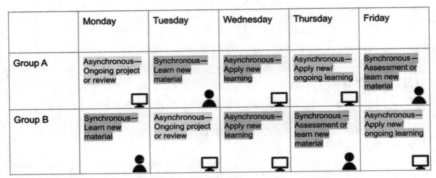

	Monday	Tuesday	Wednesday	Thursday	Friday
Group A	Asynchronous—Ongoing project or review	Synchronous—Learn new material	Asynchronous—Apply new learning	Asynchronous—Apply new/ongoing learning	Synchronous—Assessment or learn new material
Group B	Synchronous—Learn new material	Asynchronous—Ongoing project or review	Asynchronous—Apply new learning	Synchronous—Assessment or learn new material	Asynchronous—Apply new/ongoing learning

Figure 20.8: Sample schedule for alternating instruction.

This could also be achieved by recording the lesson as you teach it live and then posting it for your students to engage in from home on a slight delay. (Ideal for students who are homebound because of injury, illness, or weather.)

- **Concurrent Instruction**

Another version of coordinating lessons for your groups of students would be to live-stream the direct instruction given in the classroom for the students who are at home, so that they can participate in real-time.

A great resource for livestream teaching is **Swivl**, a docking station for your camera that allows it to move around the room with the teacher via a wearable motion detection device. And using your phone, Airpods, or a radio frequency **[RF] wireless microphone** as your microphone would allow you to move around the room as you teach.

If classwork is done on collaborative documents, students at home can easily collaborate with students in the classroom.

Trying to manage your students in the classroom and online might be more than most teachers are willing to take on, but for the adventurous teacher this option could solve the problem of creating multiple versions of the same lesson.

I also predict recording and live-streaming lessons will become a more common practice in education to account for weather events, absent students, and rural families.

RESOURCES

Items in **bold** in the text are listed here in the Resources. Direct access to all the following resources is available at https://hybridteacherresource.com and on this book's page on www.wiley.com.

PSD Global Academy—https://pga.psdschools.org

Springs Studio—https://www.d49.org/springsstudio

Swivl—https://www.swivl.com

RF Wireless microphone—https://www.amazon.com/Wireless-Microphone-System-KIMAFUN-Transmitter/dp/B074MBD643/ref=sr_1_5

Appendix: Additional References

Beeland, W. D. Jr. (n.d.). Student engagement, visual learning and technology: Can interactive whiteboards help? vtext.valdosta.edu/xmlui/bitstream/handle/10428/1252/beeland_am.pdf?sequence=1&isAllowed=y (accessed 22 February 2021).

Bialik, M. (2015, November 5). Meta-earning: The importance of thinking about thinking. https://www.learningandthebrain.com/blog/meta-learning/ (accessed 22 February 2021).

Bloom's taxonomy: Resource for educators. www.bloomstaxonomy.net (accessed 22 February 2021).

Dawson, P. (n.d.). Some thoughts for teachers on helping teenagers develop task initiation. *Smart But Scattered Kids*. https://www.smartbutscatteredkids.com/wp-content/uploads/Some-Thoughts-on-Task-Initiation.pdf (accessed 22 February 2021).

Dong, C. (2007). Positive emotions and learning: What makes a difference in multimedia design? Doctoral dissertation. New York University. Retrieved from Dissertations & Theses Database.

Dwyer, K., Bingham, S. G., Carlson, R. E. et al. (2004). Communication and connectedness in the classroom: Development of the connected classroom climate inventory. *Communication Research Reports* 21 (3): 268–272.

How do I assess student learning online? *Teachology*. www.teachology.ca/knowledgebase/how-do-i-assess-student-learning-online/ (accessed 22 February 2021).

Johnston, P. H. (2004). *Choice Words: How Our Language Affects Children's Learning*. Portland, ME: Stenhouse.

Larson, K. A. and Gerber, M. M. (1987). Effects of social metacognitive training for enhancing overt behavior in learning disabled and low achieving delinquents. *Exceptional Children* 54 (3): 201–211.

Mayer, R. and Moreno, R. (2003). Nine ways to reduce cognitive load in multimedia learning. *Educational Psychologist* 38 (1): 43–52. https://www .theurbanclimatologist.com/uploads/4/4/2/5/44250401/mayermoreno-2003reducingcognitiveoverload.pdf (accessed 22 February 2021).

Meiklejohn, J., Phillips, C., Freedman, M. L. et al. (2012). Integrating mindfulness training into K-12 education. *Mindfulness* 3: 291–307. https://link.springer. com/article/10.1007%252Fs12671-012-0094-5 (accessed 22 February 2021).

Noonoo, S. (2020, March 20). Here's what schools can do for the millions of students without internet access. *EdSurge.* https://www.edsurge.com/ news/2020-03-20-here-s-what-schools-can-do-for-the-millions-of-students-without-internet-access (accessed 22 February 2021).

Perry, B. (n.d.). Neuroscience and the brain. *Child Trauma Academy.* www .childtrauma.org (accessed 3 March 2021).

Sorden, S. (2012). The cognitive theory of multimedia learning. https:// sorden.com/portfolio/sorden_draft_multimedia2012.pdf (accessed 22 February 2021).

Spencer, J. (2019, April 6). What is design thinking? https://spencerauthor.com/ what-is-design-thinking/ (accessed 22 February 2021).

Student privacy laws: What district & school administrators need to know. *Education Framework.* https://educationframework.com/resources/student-privacy-laws/federal-laws (accessed 22 February 2021).

Williams, P. (2017). Student agency for powerful learning. *Knowledge Quest* 45 (4): 8–15. https://files.eric.ed.gov/fulltext/EJ1136307.pdf (accessed 22 February 2021).

Winkelmes, M. (2013, Spring). Transparency in teaching: Faculty share data and improve students' learning. *Liberal Education* 99 (2): 48–55. See also Illinois Initiative on Transparency in Learning and Teaching, https://www.aacu.org/ publications-research/periodicals/transparency-teaching-faculty-share-data-and-improve-students.

Index

Page numbers followed by *f* refer to figures.

E

W

Y